UNLOCKING REAL ESTATE WEALTH:

A Comprehensive Guide to Strategic Investing and Property Management

BY

John M. Woods

About The Author

John M. Woods, a financial virtuoso hailing from the bustling streets of New York City, stands as a beacon of wisdom in the realm of business and finance. With a mysterious air that accompanies his every move, Woods has etched his name into the annals of financial literature, captivating readers with his enigmatic charm and unparalleled insights.

Table of Contents

INTRODUCTION   9
Why Invest In Real Estate   9
Overview Of Real Estate Markets   10
Chapter 1   13
Foundations of Real Estate Investing   13
Defining your investment objectives   20
Assessing your risk tolerance   24
Establishing a realistic budget   31
Chapter 2   39
Strategic Property Selection   39
Researching profitable markets   43
Evaluating Neighborhoods and Growth Potential   47
Property Types: Residential, Commercial, and
Beyond   51
Chapter 3   59
Financial Planning for Real Estate   59
Understanding mortgage options   64
Exploring financing strategies   69
Budgeting for maintenance and upkeep   74
Chapter 4   81
Building a diverse portfolio   81
Benefits of diversification   88
Balancing high and low-risk investments   94
Incorporating Real Estate Investment Trusts (REITs)
101
Chapter 5   107
Navigating the Buying Process in Real Estate   107

1. Steps in the Real Estate Purchase: 107

2. Negotiation Techniques for Buyers: 109

3. Due Diligence and Property Inspection: 111

Chapter 6   113

Effective Property Management   113

1. Tenant Screening and Selection: 114

2. Lease Agreement Best Practices: 116

3. Property Maintenance and Value Enhancement:
118

Chapter 7   121

Maximizing Returns   121

Rental Income Strategies   123

House Flipping Techniques: 127

Leveraging Tax Incentives: 132

Chapter 8   137

Addressing Challenges and Risks: 137

Mitigating market fluctuations   143

Managing Economic Downturns   147

Strategies for Handling Property Challenges   151

Chapter 9   157

Legal and Regulatory Considerations   157

Understanding Real Estate Laws   161

Navigating Zoning Regulations   166

Tax implications and strategies   170

Chapter 10   173

Long-term wealth building   173

Retirement planning through real estate   177

Legacy planning and generational wealth   180

Real estate as a passive income source   184

Chapter 11   189
Staying Informed and Adapting   189
Keeping Abreast of Market Trends   191
Adapting Strategies to Market Changes   196
Continuing education in real estate   201
Conclusion   205
REVIEW PAGE   209

INTRODUCTION

Welcome to "Unlocking Real Estate Wealth: A Comprehensive Guide to Strategic Investing and Property Management." In the dynamic landscape of real estate, the potential for wealth creation and financial growth is vast, but so are the complexities and challenges. Whether you are a seasoned investor looking to refine your strategies or a novice eager to embark on your first real estate venture, this guide is your roadmap to navigating the intricate nuances of strategic investing and effective property management.

Why Invest In Real Estate

The allure of real estate lies not only in the tangible nature of property but also in its capacity to generate consistent income, build long-term equity, and serve as a cornerstone for financial stability. This comprehensive guide aims to demystify the process, providing you with the knowledge, tools, and insights needed to make informed decisions, mitigate risks, and cultivate a successful real estate portfolio.

As we journey through the chapters, we'll explore the fundamental principles of real estate investing, from defining your investment objectives to navigating the complexities of property selection, financing, and the intricacies of property management. We'll delve into the art of strategic decision-making, equipping you with the skills to assess markets, identify lucrative opportunities, and build a diversified portfolio that stands the test of time.

Overview Of Real Estate Markets

Effective property management is a crucial aspect of real estate success, and this guide will illuminate best practices for tenant selection, lease agreements, and maintaining property value. From maximizing returns through rental income strategies to addressing challenges and mitigating risks, each chapter is crafted to provide actionable insights that empower you to make sound, informed decisions.

Legal and regulatory considerations are integral to real estate endeavors, and we'll unravel the complexities of real estate laws, zoning regulations, and tax implications, ensuring you navigate these crucial aspects with confidence and compliance.

Long-term wealth building is the ultimate goal, and we'll explore how real estate can be a powerful vehicle for retirement planning, legacy creation, and the generation of passive income. Staying informed and adaptable is key in the ever-evolving real estate landscape, and our guide concludes with strategies to keep you abreast of market trends and continue your journey towards real estate success.

Whether you're envisioning your first property investment or seeking to refine your existing portfolio, "Unlocking Real Estate Wealth" is your comprehensive guide to making strategic, informed decisions that unlock the full potential of real estate as a wealth-building asset. Let's embark on this journey together, unlocking the doors to a world of real estate opportunities and financial prosperity.

Chapter 1

Foundations of Real Estate Investing

Real estate investing is an endeavor that involves the acquisition, ownership, management, rental, or sale of real estate for profit. It has long been considered one of the most enduring and potentially lucrative investment strategies available. Understanding the foundations of real estate investing is crucial for anyone looking to enter this field. This comprehensive guide aims to explore the fundamental principles, strategies, and considerations essential for a successful and sustainable real estate investment.

Overview of Real Estate Investing

Real estate investing encompasses various forms of properties, including residential, commercial, industrial, and land. Investors typically engage in real estate transactions with the primary goal of generating income, either through rental income, capital appreciation, or both. Unlike other investment vehicles such as stocks or bonds, real estate offers unique advantages like tangible assets, leverage, and potential tax benefits.

Key Principles of Real Estate Investing

1. Market Knowledge: Understanding the local real estate market is essential. Factors such as supply and demand, economic trends, demographics, and zoning regulations can significantly impact the performance of real estate investments.

2. Risk Management: Real estate investments carry inherent risks, including market fluctuations, property damage, and liability

issues. Assessing and mitigating these risks through proper due diligence and risk management strategies are paramount.

3. Financial Analysis: Evaluating the financial viability of a real estate investment involves analyzing factors such as cash flow projections, property appreciation potential, operating expenses, financing options, and return on investment (ROI).

4. Property Valuation: Accurately valuing a property is critical to making informed investment decisions. Various methods, including comparative market analysis, income approach, and cost approach, are used to determine the fair market value of real estate.

Types of Real Estate Investments

1. Residential Real Estate: This category includes single-family homes, condominiums, townhouses, and multifamily

properties. Residential real estate investments often focus on rental income and long-term capital appreciation.

2. Commercial Real Estate: Commercial properties such as office buildings, retail spaces, industrial facilities, and warehouses cater to businesses and typically offer higher rental yields but may involve more complex leasing agreements and property management.

3. Real Estate Investment Trusts (REITs): REITs allow investors to gain exposure to real estate by investing in publicly traded companies that own, operate, or finance income-generating properties. REITs offer liquidity and diversification in real estate investments.

4. Land Development: Land investment involves purchasing undeveloped or underdeveloped land with the intention of adding value through subdivision,

entitlements, rezoning, or development for residential, commercial, or industrial purposes.

Real Estate Investment Strategies

1. Buy and Hold: A long-term strategy involving the acquisition of properties with the intention of renting them out to generate consistent rental income and benefit from property appreciation over time.

2. Fix and Flip: This strategy involves purchasing distressed properties, renovating or improving them, and selling for a profit in a relatively short period. Successful execution requires careful cost analysis and market knowledge.

3. Wholesaling: Involves securing properties at below-market prices and assigning the purchase contract to another investor for a fee, often without taking ownership of the

property. Effective marketing and negotiation skills are essential for this strategy.

4. Airbnb and Short-Term Rentals: Leveraging platforms like Airbnb to rent out properties for short-term stays can yield higher rental income but requires compliance with local regulations and additional operational considerations.

Considerations for Real Estate Investors

1. Financing Options: Understanding various financing options such as conventional mortgages, hard money loans, private money, and creative financing techniques is crucial for structuring real estate deals effectively.

2. Tax Implications: Real estate investments entail specific tax considerations related to rental income, property depreciation, capital gains, and deductions for expenses like mortgage interest, property taxes, and maintenance costs.

3. Property Management: Efficient property management is essential for maintaining and enhancing the value of real estate assets. Investors can choose between self-management, hiring a professional property management company, or a hybrid approach based on their preferences and capabilities.

4. Legal and Regulatory Compliance: Real estate investing involves adherence to a myriad of laws and regulations governing property ownership, landlord-tenant relationships, fair housing practices, and property disclosures.

5. Exit Strategies: Having clear exit strategies for real estate investments, whether through selling, refinancing, or 1031 exchanges, is vital for achieving investment objectives and optimizing returns.

The foundations of real estate investing encompass a broad spectrum of principles, strategies, and considerations that form the bedrock of successful real estate ventures. Whether an individual chooses to engage in residential rentals, commercial properties, or alternative real estate investment vehicles like REITs, understanding the market, conducting thorough due diligence, and implementing sound investment strategies are essential for long-term success. By grasping the fundamental principles outlined in this guide, aspiring real estate investors can embark on their journey with confidence and a deeper understanding of the dynamic and rewarding world of real estate

Defining your investment objectives

Defining your investment objectives is a crucial step in creating a clear and effective strategy for building wealth and achieving your financial goals. This process involves identifying and articulating what you aim to accomplish with your investments, which can vary widely from person to person based on individual circumstances, risk tolerance, and time horizon. Here are key considerations when defining your investment objectives:

1. Establishing Clear Goals: Start by determining your short-term and long-term financial aspirations. These could include objectives such as funding a comfortable retirement, purchasing a home, financing education expenses, or achieving specific lifestyle goals. By outlining these goals, you can begin to tailor your investment approach to align with your specific needs.

2. Risk Tolerance: Assessing your comfort level with investment risk is essential. Some individuals may be willing to take on higher levels of risk in pursuit of potentially higher returns, while others may prioritize capital preservation and seek more conservative investment options. Understanding your risk

tolerance will help guide your asset allocation and investment choices.

3. Time Horizon: Consider the timeframe over which you intend to achieve your investment objectives. Short-term goals may require a more conservative investment approach, while long-term goals could allow for a more aggressive investment strategy, given the potential for greater market fluctuations to even out over time.

4. Return Expectations: Clarify the level of return you anticipate from your investments. While it's important to be realistic about potential returns, having a target in mind can help guide your investment decisions and provide a benchmark against which to measure performance.

5. Liquidity Needs: Assess how quickly you may need to access your investment funds. Understanding your liquidity requirements can influence the types of investments you

choose, as some assets may be more easily converted to cash than others.

6. Diversification: Consider the benefits of diversifying your portfolio across different asset classes, industries, and geographic regions. Diversification can help mitigate risk and optimize the potential for achieving your investment objectives.

7. Tax Considerations: Factor in the impact of taxes on your investment returns. Strategies such as contributing to tax-advantaged accounts or structuring investments with tax efficiency in mind can help maximize after-tax returns.

8. Regular Review: Investment objectives are not static and may evolve over time due to changes in personal circumstances, market conditions, or economic factors. Regularly reviewing and potentially adjusting your investment objectives ensures that your

investment strategy remains aligned with your current needs and goals.

By clearly defining your investment objectives, you lay the foundation for constructing a personalized investment plan that supports your financial aspirations. Professional financial advisors can provide valuable guidance in this process, helping you assess your objectives and develop a customized investment strategy tailored to your unique situation.

Assessing your risk tolerance

Assessing your risk tolerance is a critical step in the investment process, as it helps determine the level of investment risk you are comfortable with and willing to accept. Risk tolerance is a personal measure that reflects an individual's ability to endure market fluctuations and potential investment losses without experiencing undue stress or anxiety, assessing your risk tolerance involves understanding the various levels of risk and how they may align with different investment strategies. Let's explore some of them ;

Risk Profiles: Investors generally fall into one of three risk profiles - conservative, moderate, or aggressive. A conservative investor prioritizes capital preservation and typically seeks lower-risk investments with more stable returns, such as bonds and money market funds. A moderate investor seeks a balance between potential returns and risk, often favoring a diversified mix of stocks, bonds, and other assets. An aggressive investor is willing to accept higher levels of risk in pursuit of potentially higher returns and may focus on growth-oriented investments such as individual stocks and emerging market funds.

Quantitative vs. Qualitative Assessments: When evaluating risk tolerance, it's important to consider both quantitative and qualitative factors. Quantitative assessments may involve numerical measurements of an investor's financial situation, such as income, assets, and liabilities, to determine their capacity for risk. Qualitative assessments, on the other hand, may involve understanding an investor's psychological attitude towards risk, emotional responses to market fluctuations, and personal beliefs about investing.

Risk Capacity vs. Risk Tolerance: It's essential to distinguish between risk capacity and risk tolerance. Risk capacity refers to an investor's financial ability to take on risk, considering factors such as income, expenses, and time horizon. Risk tolerance, on the other hand, reflects an investor's emotional comfort with risk and market volatility. Both factors play a crucial role in shaping an individual's overall risk profile and investment approach.

Behavioral Finance: Delving into the realm of behavioral finance can provide valuable insights into how individuals perceive and respond to investment risk. Behavioral biases, such as loss aversion (the tendency to strongly prefer avoiding losses over acquiring gains) and overconfidence, can influence risk tolerance and investment decision-making. Understanding these behavioral tendencies can help investors better navigate market uncertainties and make more disciplined choices.

Dynamic Nature of Risk Tolerance: It's important to recognize that risk tolerance is not static and can evolve over time. Life events, such as marriage, starting a family, changing careers, or nearing retirement, can impact an individual's risk tolerance. Additionally, market experiences, economic conditions, and personal financial milestones can also influence how comfortable an investor feels with different levels of risk.

Points to consider when evaluating your risk tolerance

1. Personal Circumstances: Begin by evaluating your current financial situation, including your income, expenses, debts, and any other financial obligations. Understanding your financial capacity to withstand investment losses is an essential aspect of assessing risk tolerance.

2. Investment Experience: Consider your familiarity and experience with different types of investments. Investors with more exposure to various asset classes may be more comfortable taking on higher levels of risk, while those with limited investment experience may prefer a more conservative approach.

3. Emotional Response: Reflect on how you typically react to market volatility and fluctuations in the value of your investments. If the idea of potential losses causes

significant stress or anxiety, it may indicate a lower risk tolerance.

4. Time Horizon: Assess the length of time over which you intend to hold your investments. Long-term investors may have a greater capacity to endure short-term market fluctuations, allowing them to consider riskier assets, whereas individuals with shorter time horizons may lean towards more conservative investments.

5. Financial Goals: Your specific financial goals can also influence your risk tolerance. For instance, if you are saving for retirement and have several decades before you'll need the funds, you may be more open to taking on higher levels of risk to potentially secure higher returns.

6. Diversification: Consider the role of diversification in managing risk. By spreading your investments across different asset classes and regions, you can reduce the

impact of poor performance from any single investment on your overall portfolio.

7. Professional Guidance: Seeking advice from a knowledgeable financial advisor can provide valuable insights into your risk tolerance. Advisors may use questionnaires and other tools to help gauge your risk tolerance and align your investment strategy with your comfort level.

Dynamic Nature of Risk Tolerance: It's important to recognize that risk tolerance is not static and can evolve over time. Life events, such as marriage, starting a family, changing careers, or nearing retirement, can impact an individual's risk tolerance. Additionally, market experiences, economic conditions, and personal financial milestones can also influence how comfortable an investor feels with different levels of risk. Regularly reassessing your risk tolerance ensures that your investment strategy remains aligned with your comfort level and financial objectives.

By carefully considering these factors and seeking guidance when needed, you can gain a clearer understanding of your risk tolerance and make well-informed investment decisions that align with your unique financial situation and goals.

Establishing a realistic budget

Establishing a realistic budget is a fundamental aspect of personal financial management. It involves creating a detailed plan that outlines income and expenditures to ensure that spending aligns with financial goals. Let's explore the steps involved in creating and understanding a realistic budget.

1. Assess Your Income: The first step in establishing a realistic budget is to identify and quantify all sources of income. This includes salaries, wages, bonuses, freelance

earnings, investment returns, and any other incoming funds. Understanding your total monthly or annual income provides a clear starting point for managing your finances.

2. Track Your Expenses: It's essential to track and categorize all expenses to gain a comprehensive understanding of where your money is going. This includes fixed expenses such as rent or mortgage payments, utilities, insurance, and loan repayments, as well as variable expenses like groceries, dining out, entertainment, and discretionary purchases. Tools like budgeting apps or spreadsheets can help organize and analyze spending habits.

3. Differentiate Between Needs and Wants: Distinguishing between essential needs and discretionary wants is crucial when creating a budget. Needs are necessary expenses essential for sustaining your lifestyle, such as housing, food, transportation, and healthcare. Wants, on the other hand, encompass

non-essential spending on items like vacations, luxury goods, and entertainment. Prioritizing needs over wants ensures that essential expenses are consistently covered before allocating funds to discretionary items.

4. Set Realistic Goals: When establishing a budget, it's important to set realistic financial goals based on your income and expenditure patterns. Whether it's saving for a down payment on a home, paying off debt, building an emergency fund, or investing for retirement, defining achievable objectives helps guide your budgeting decisions.

5. Consider Irregular Expenses: In addition to monthly bills, budgeting should account for periodic or irregular expenses, such as annual insurance premiums, vehicle maintenance, or holiday expenses. Allocating a portion of your income towards these irregular costs

helps prevent unexpected financial strain when they arise.

6. Create a Budget Allocation Plan: Once you have a clear overview of your income and expenses, allocate specific amounts to each spending category based on your financial priorities. This may involve setting aside a certain percentage for savings, allocating a fixed amount for discretionary spending, and ensuring that all essential expenses are covered.

7. Review and Adjust Regularly: A realistic budget is not static; it requires regular review and adjustment to reflect changes in income, expenses, and financial goals. Circumstances such as salary increases, job transitions, relocation, or major life events may necessitate modifications to your budget to ensure it remains aligned with your current financial situation.

Additionally,

1. Emergency Fund Provision: A realistic budget should include provisions for building an emergency fund. This fund acts as a financial safety net, providing a buffer against unexpected expenses or income disruptions such as medical emergencies, car repairs, or temporary unemployment. Setting aside a portion of your income specifically for this purpose is crucial for financial security and stability.

2. Debt Management: Managing existing debt and avoiding accumulating further debt is an integral part of budgeting. Including a strategy for reducing and eliminating high-interest debt in your budget is essential. This may involve allocating extra funds towards debt repayment or consolidating debts to lower interest rates, ultimately freeing up more resources for savings and investments.

3. Long-Term Planning: Realistic budgeting extends beyond immediate financial needs and encompasses long-term planning. This includes saving for retirement, investing in education or career development, and making provisions for significant life events such as buying a home, starting a family, or caring for aging relatives. A well-structured budget allocates resources towards long-term goals, enabling individuals to build wealth and secure their financial future.

4. Flexibility and Adaptability: While setting a budget is important, it is equally vital to recognize that life circumstances can change. Therefore, a realistic budget should allow for flexibility and adaptability. Unexpected expenses, changes in income, or shifts in priorities may require adjustments to the budget. Embracing the need for flexibility ensures that the budget remains relevant and sustainable in varying situations.

5. Behavioral Economics and Psychology: Understanding the behavioral aspects of personal finance plays a significant role in establishing a realistic budget. Recognizing patterns of impulse spending, emotional triggers for financial decisions, and the impact of cognitive biases on money management can inform the creation of a budget that aligns with individual behavior and motivates positive financial habits.

6. Continuous Learning and Improvement: Establishing a realistic budget is an ongoing process that benefits from continuous learning and improvement. Engaging in financial literacy education, seeking advice from financial professionals, and staying informed about economic trends and market conditions can enhance budgeting skills and decision-making.

By following these steps, individuals can establish a realistic budget that serves as a practical financial roadmap. A well-constructed budget provides clarity, discipline, and control over personal finances, fostering responsible spending habits and promoting progress towards achieving long-term financial objectives.

Chapter 2

Strategic Property Selection

Strategic property selection involves the careful consideration and evaluation of various factors to identify and acquire real estate assets that align with specific investment goals, financial objectives, and long-term plans. It encompasses a systematic approach to analyzing potential properties, understanding market dynamics, and making informed decisions to maximize returns and mitigate risks.

Key Elements of Strategic Property Selection:

1. Investment Objectives: Before selecting a property, it is crucial to define clear investment objectives. These objectives may include generating rental income, achieving

capital appreciation, diversifying a portfolio, or providing a hedge against inflation. Understanding these goals helps in identifying properties that best fit the intended investment strategy.

2. Location Analysis: Location plays a pivotal role in property selection. Factors such as neighborhood demographics, proximity to amenities, economic trends, and development potential can significantly impact the property's value and income potential. Conducting thorough research on the local market dynamics and growth prospects helps in identifying areas with strong rental demand or potential for future appreciation.

3. Property Type and Market Segment: Different property types (residential, commercial, industrial, etc.) and market segments (luxury, affordable housing, retail, office space, etc.) exhibit distinct

characteristics and performance metrics. Evaluating the suitability of a property type and market segment in relation to the investment strategy is essential for strategic property selection.

4. Financial Analysis: A comprehensive financial analysis is critical in assessing the investment potential of a property. This analysis involves evaluating the acquisition costs, operating expenses, potential rental income, cash flow projections, and overall return on investment. Additionally, considering financing options, loan terms, and interest rates helps in determining the affordability and viability of the investment.

5. Risk Assessment and Mitigation: Identifying and mitigating potential risks associated with a property investment is an integral part of strategic property selection. This includes evaluating factors such as market volatility, tenant turnover, regulatory

changes, and property-specific risks. Implementing risk mitigation strategies, such as diversifying across properties or choosing properties with stable income streams, can help safeguard the investment.

6. Exit Strategy: Having a clear exit strategy is essential when selecting properties, especially for investors looking to capitalize on short-term opportunities or plan for future liquidity. Understanding potential exit routes, such as resale, refinancing, or repositioning the property, contributes to strategic decision-making and long-term portfolio management.

Strategic property selection requires a holistic approach that combines financial analysis, market research, risk assessment, and a deep understanding of investment goals. By carefully evaluating the aforementioned elements, investors can make informed decisions that align with their specific investment criteria and contribute to building a resilient and profitable real estate portfolio. Ultimately, strategic property selection balances the pursuit of attractive returns with prudent risk management, enabling investors to optimize their real estate investments and achieve long-term financial success.

Researching profitable markets

Researching profitable markets involves the systematic analysis of various factors to identify and assess investment opportunities that offer attractive returns and growth potential. Whether it's real estate, stocks, or other investment vehicles, thorough market research is crucial for making informed decisions and maximizing investment profitability. Here are key steps and considerations for researching profitable markets:

1. Market Analysis: Understanding the broader market dynamics is essential. This includes analyzing economic indicators, industry trends, consumer behavior, and demographic shifts. By keeping abreast of macroeconomic developments, investors can identify sectors and markets with strong growth prospects and favorable investment conditions.

2. Sector and Industry Research: Delving into specific sectors and industries helps in pinpointing areas of opportunity. Examining market trends, competitive landscape, regulatory environment, and technological advancements provides insights into sectors with high growth potential and profitability.

3. Geographic Considerations: For real estate and certain businesses, location is a critical factor. Researching geographic areas with robust economic activity, population growth, and infrastructure development can lead to

identifying promising markets for investment.

4. Competitive Analysis: Evaluating existing competitors and market players is crucial. Understanding their market share, pricing strategies, product offerings, and customer base can help in assessing the feasibility and competitiveness of entering a particular market.

5. Consumer Demand and Behavior: Understanding consumer preferences, spending patterns, and evolving needs is vital in identifying markets with strong demand for products or services. Consumer behavior analysis can provide valuable insights into emerging trends and market niches.

6. Regulatory and Legal Environment: Researching the regulatory and legal framework governing a market is essential. Knowledge of regulations, tax policies, licensing requirements, and compliance

standards helps in assessing the operational and investment risks associated with a particular market.

7. Risk Assessment: Identifying and mitigating potential risks is an integral part of researching profitable markets. Factors such as market volatility, political instability, currency fluctuations, and environmental risks should be thoroughly evaluated to gauge the overall risk-reward profile of an investment.

8. Performance Metrics: Using performance metrics such as return on investment (ROI), market growth rates, price-to-earnings ratio (P/E ratio), and other financial indicators can aid in comparing and evaluating the potential profitability of different markets.

Researching profitable markets involves a multi-faceted approach that integrates economic, industry-specific, and consumer-related analyses. Through comprehensive market research, investors can identify high-potential markets, assess risk factors, and make data-driven investment decisions. Utilizing a combination of qualitative and quantitative research methods provides a holistic view of market opportunities, allowing investors to capitalize on profitable ventures while managing associated risks. By staying informed and continuously refining their market research approach, investors can position themselves for successful and profitable investments in dynamic and evolving markets.

Evaluating Neighborhoods and Growth Potential

Evaluating neighborhoods for growth potential involves assessing various factors that can influence the desirability and investment prospects of a specific area. This evaluation is crucial for real estate investors, businesses, and individuals looking to make informed decisions about where to live or invest. Here are key steps and considerations for evaluating neighborhoods and their growth potential:

1. Economic Indicators: Researching the economic health of a neighborhood is essential. This includes evaluating factors such as employment opportunities, income levels, economic diversification, and future development projects. Strong economic indicators often correlate with growth potential and increased property values.

2. Demographic Trends: Analyzing demographic data provides insights into population growth, age distribution, household income, and lifestyle preferences within a neighborhood. Changes in demographics, such as an influx of younger residents or increasing affluence, can signify growth potential and increased demand for goods and services.

3. Infrastructure and Amenities: Assessing the quality of infrastructure, transportation connectivity, public services, and proximity to amenities (schools, parks, shopping centers) is crucial. Neighborhoods with well-developed infrastructure and access to desirable amenities are often more attractive to residents and have higher growth potential.

4. Real Estate Market Trends: Monitoring real estate market trends within a neighborhood, such as property values, rental rates, and market activity, helps in gauging the investment potential. A neighborhood with rising property values and low vacancy rates may indicate strong growth potential.

5. Regulatory Environment: Understanding local zoning laws, development regulations, and urban planning initiatives is important for assessing growth potential. Areas with favorable development policies and urban revitalization projects may experience

positive growth and appreciation in property values.

6. School District Quality: The quality of local schools can significantly influence neighborhood desirability and, consequently, growth potential. Areas with well-regarded schools often attract families and contribute to a stable and appreciating real estate market.

7. Crime Rates and Safety: Evaluating neighborhood safety and crime rates is vital. Lower crime rates and a strong sense of community security not only make a neighborhood more appealing but also positively impact its growth potential.

Evaluating neighborhoods for growth potential involves a comprehensive assessment of economic, demographic, infrastructural, and market-related factors. By considering these key factors, investors, businesses, and homebuyers can gauge the attractiveness and potential of a neighborhood for long-term growth and investment. Furthermore, understanding the regulatory environment, educational opportunities, and safety aspects provides a holistic view of the neighborhood's livability and future prospects. This thorough evaluation helps stakeholders make informed decisions that align with their investment objectives and residential preferences, ultimately positioning them to benefit from the growth and development potential of a chosen neighborhood.

Property Types: Residential, Commercial, and Beyond

Property types encompass a diverse range of real estate assets, each serving distinct purposes and catering to specific needs. The main categories of property types include residential, commercial, industrial, and mixed-use properties. Here, I will delve into the primary property types of residential and commercial, explaining their characteristics, uses, and investment considerations:

Residential Properties:

Residential properties are designed for human habitation and can be further classified into single-family homes, multi-family dwellings, condominiums, townhouses, and apartment buildings.

Single-Family Homes: These detached houses are occupied by a single household and offer privacy, personalized space, and often a yard or outdoor area. They are popular among homeowners seeking autonomy and independence.

Multi-Family Dwellings: This category includes properties having units for multiple households within a single building or complex. Apartment buildings, duplexes, triplexes, and quadplexes fall under this category.

Condominiums: Commonly known as condos, these units are individually owned within a larger development with shared common areas and amenities. Condos offer a blend of ownership and maintenance convenience.

Townhouses: Typically designed as multi-level properties that share walls with adjacent units, townhouses offer a balance between the independence of a single-family home and the convenience of communal maintenance.

Apartment Buildings: These properties consist of multiple rental units, ranging from small complexes to high-rise buildings, providing housing for diverse demographics, including students, professionals, and families.

Residential property investment considerations revolve around factors such as location, rental demand, neighborhood development, property management, and long-term potential for appreciation. Investors should also assess aspects like local school quality, proximity to amenities, and community safety when evaluating residential properties.

Commercial Properties:

Commercial properties are used for business and income-generating purposes and can encompass various subcategories, including office buildings, retail spaces, industrial facilities, hospitality properties, and mixed-use developments.

Office Buildings: These properties are tailored for professional and administrative activities, such as corporate offices, coworking spaces, and business centers. Classifications based on size, location, and tenant profile can further segment the office property market.

Retail Spaces: Retail properties encompass shopping centers, standalone stores, restaurants, and other businesses focused on consumer goods and services. The success of retail properties is closely linked to demographics, foot traffic, and consumer spending patterns.

Industrial Facilities: Industrial properties encompass warehouses, manufacturing plants, distribution centers, and industrial parks. Factors such as proximity to transportation networks, logistics infrastructure, and workforce availability are critical for industrial property evaluations.

Hospitality Properties: This category includes hotels, motels, resorts, and other lodging establishments. Revenue generation in the hospitality sector is influenced by tourism trends, location attractiveness, and the overall travel and leisure industry.

Mixed-Use Developments: These properties combine residential, commercial, and often retail components within a single complex or neighborhood, fostering integrated living, working, and recreational environments.

Commercial property investment considerations center on factors such as tenant creditworthiness, lease terms, market demand, property maintenance, and zoning regulations. Location, accessibility, and visibility are pivotal in assessing the potential success of commercial properties.

Beyond Residential and Commercial Real Estate:

Beyond residential and commercial properties, other property types include industrial real estate, which comprises manufacturing, warehouse, and distribution facilities. Additionally, mixed-use properties integrate residential, commercial, and sometimes industrial components, offering a diverse and convenient urban lifestyle. Specialized real estate assets such as healthcare facilities, educational institutions, recreational properties, and agricultural land also constitute distinct property types with unique investment dynamics and operational considerations.

Understanding the nuances of different property types enables investors, developers, and property owners to make informed decisions aligned with their investment objectives and risk tolerance. Whether considering residential properties for stable rental income or exploring commercial opportunities for business growth, a thorough understanding of property types and their respective dynamics is essential for successful real estate ventures.

Chapter 3

Financial Planning for Real Estate

Financial planning for real estate is a comprehensive process that involves strategically managing one's finances to achieve specific real estate-related goals. This can encompass various aspects, including budgeting, saving, investment strategies, risk management, tax planning, and ongoing financial management. Let's explore each of these components in greater depth:

1. Setting Realistic Goals:

Financial planning for real estate begins with establishing clear and achievable objectives. These may include purchasing a primary residence, acquiring rental properties for passive income, or diversifying an investment portfolio with real estate assets. Identifying both long-term and short-term goals is crucial in creating a roadmap for financial planning.

2. Budgeting and Saving:

Creating a comprehensive budget is essential for understanding current financial positions and identifying potential areas for saving. It involves tracking income, expenses, and setting aside a portion of the income for future real estate investments. Saving is critical for accumulating the initial capital required for down payments, closing costs, and other associated expenses.

3. Understanding Mortgage Options:

For many individuals, obtaining a mortgage is a necessary step in purchasing real estate. Thus, understanding the various mortgage options available, including fixed-rate mortgages, adjustable-rate mortgages, and government-backed loans, is crucial. Factors such as interest rates, loan terms, and down payment requirements need to be carefully considered in the context of the individual's financial situation.

4. Risk Management:

Real estate investments come with inherent risks such as market volatility, property depreciation, and unexpected expenses. Financial planning involves assessing and mitigating these risks. This may include strategies such as diversification of real estate holdings, maintaining adequate insurance coverage, and creating emergency funds to address unforeseen expenses.

5. Tax Planning:

Real estate investments have significant tax implications. Financial planning includes understanding the tax advantages and obligations associated with real estate ownership. This may involve utilizing tax-efficient investment vehicles, taking advantage of deductions, and complying with tax regulations related to rental income, capital gains, and property taxes.

6. Investing in Real Estate:

Financial planning requires determining how to allocate funds for real estate investments based on individual risk tolerance, investment horizon, and financial goals. This may include evaluating direct property purchases, investing in real estate investment trusts (REITs), or exploring other real estate-related securities. It also involves understanding the liquidity, potential returns, and associated risks of different real estate investment options.

7. Estate Planning:

Real estate assets are a fundamental part of an individual's estate. Proper estate planning ensures that real estate holdings are transferred according to the owner's wishes upon death and may involve strategies to minimize estate taxes. This may include creating wills, establishing trusts, and considering the implications of real estate inheritance on the overall estate plan.

8. Ongoing Financial Management:

Once real estate assets are acquired, ongoing financial management is crucial. This involves tracking income and expenses related to property ownership, ensuring adequate insurance coverage, making informed decisions regarding property improvements and renovations, and monitoring the performance of real estate investments in alignment with long-term financial goals.

Financial planning for real estate is a dynamic and personalized process that involves various considerations, including budgeting, saving, risk management, tax planning, investment strategies, estate planning, and ongoing financial management. Developing a comprehensive financial plan for real estate requires a deep understanding of an individual's financial circumstances, long-term goals, and the complexities inherent in the real estate market. Seeking guidance from financial advisors and real estate professionals can provide valuable support in creating and executing a sound financial plan for real estate.

Understanding mortgage options

Understanding mortgage options is crucial for individuals considering real estate investments or purchasing a home. Mortgages, being long-term commitments, significantly impact personal finances, making it essential to comprehend the available options. Let's explore the key aspects of understanding mortgage options in greater depth:

1. Fixed-Rate Mortgages:

A fixed-rate mortgage offers a set interest rate and consistent monthly payments throughout the loan term. This stability provides predictability, making it easier for borrowers to plan their finances. It is an ideal option when interest rates are low, as locking in a favorable rate provides protection against potential future rate increases.

2. Adjustable-Rate Mortgages (ARMs):

ARMs feature an interest rate that may fluctuate over time based on market conditions. Initial lower rates make ARMs attractive, particularly for those planning to move or refinance before any potential rate adjustments. Borrowers should carefully consider their ability to handle potentially higher payments if rates rise in the future.

3. Government-Backed Loans:

Government-backed loans, such as those offered by the Federal Housing Administration (FHA), the U.S. Department of Veterans Affairs (VA), or the U.S. Department of Agriculture (USDA), are designed to assist individuals who may not qualify for conventional mortgages. These loans often feature lower down payment requirements and more lenient credit score qualifications.

4. Conventional Mortgages:

Conventional mortgages are not insured or guaranteed by government entities. They typically require higher credit scores and down payments compared to government-backed loans. Private mortgage insurance (PMI) may be necessary for borrowers who put down less than 20% of the home's purchase price.

5. Jumbo Loans:

Jumbo loans are used to finance properties that exceed the conforming loan limits set by government-sponsored enterprises (GSEs) like Fannie Mae and Freddie Mac. As such, they generally have stricter requirements and higher interest rates due to the increased risk associated with larger loan amounts.

6. Interest-Only Mortgages:

With interest-only mortgages, borrowers pay only the interest for a specified initial period, after which they begin to pay both principal and interest. While this option can provide lower initial payments, borrowers should be prepared for potential payment increases once the interest-only period ends.

7. Balloon Mortgages:

Balloon mortgages feature low, fixed interest payments for a set period, after which the remaining balance becomes due in full, necessitating either a large final payment or refinancing. This option should be approached cautiously, as the potential need to refinance or pay a substantial lump sum poses considerable risk.

8. Understanding Closing Costs:

In addition to considering different mortgage types, understanding the associated closing costs is vital. These costs can include origination fees, appraisal fees, title insurance, and other expenses. Borrowers should carefully review and compare these costs across various lenders when evaluating mortgage options.

Understanding mortgage options is a critical component of the home buying or real estate investment process. Each mortgage type has its own advantages and risks, and selecting the right option depends on individual financial circumstances, goals, and risk tolerance. Seeking guidance from mortgage professionals and financial advisors can help individuals make informed decisions when navigating the complexities of mortgage options.

Exploring financing strategies

Exploring financing strategies is a key aspect of any financial plan, whether it involves funding a business venture, purchasing real estate, or managing personal assets. The intricate nature of financing strategies requires a comprehensive understanding of available options and their implications. Let's delve deeply into this topic to provide thorough insights:

1. Debt Financing:

Debt financing involves borrowing funds from external sources, such as banks, financial institutions, or private lenders. It typically requires repayment with interest over a specified period. This strategy can provide immediate access to capital for business expansion, investment opportunities, or major purchases, but it also comes with the obligation to manage debt payments effectively to avoid financial strain.

2. Equity Financing:

Equity financing involves raising funds by selling shares of ownership in a company or project. This approach can be attractive for entrepreneurs and businesses seeking capital without taking on debt. However, it often entails relinquishing partial ownership and potentially sharing decision-making authority with investors or shareholders.

3. Bootstrapping:

Bootstrapping refers to self-funding a venture or project without relying on external financing. While this approach minimizes debt and dilution of ownership, it may limit the scale and pace of growth due to resource constraints. Entrepreneurial endeavors often leverage personal savings, revenue reinvestment, or sweat equity as part of bootstrapping strategies.

4. Financial Leverage:

Financial leverage involves using borrowed funds to amplify potential returns on investment. This strategy can enhance profitability in favorable market conditions, but it also magnifies the risk of losses when investments underperform. Prudent use of financial leverage requires careful consideration of risk tolerance and market dynamics.

5. Mezzanine Financing:

Mezzanine financing sits between debt and equity, offering a hybrid form of capital that combines elements of both. It typically involves subordinate debt with equity features, such as warrants or conversion rights. Mezzanine financing is often used to support growth initiatives, acquisitions, or buyouts, providing flexibility and potentially higher returns compared to traditional debt instruments.

6. Crowdfunding:

Crowdfunding utilizes online platforms to raise small amounts of capital from a large number of individuals or entities. This approach has gained popularity for funding creative projects, startups, and social causes. While it can offer an alternative to traditional financing channels, successful crowdfunding campaigns require compelling narratives, targeted marketing, and engagement with a supportive community.

7. Impact Investing:

Impact investing aims to generate positive social or environmental impact alongside financial returns. Investors seek opportunities to allocate capital to businesses, organizations, or projects that address pressing societal challenges, such as sustainable development, healthcare access, or poverty alleviation. Impact investing strategies align financial goals with values-based and purpose-driven objectives.

8. Securitization:

Securitization involves pooling and packaging financial assets, such as mortgages, loans, or receivables, into tradable securities. These securities, backed by the underlying assets, can be sold to investors in the secondary market. Securitization plays a pivotal role in diversifying funding sources for financial institutions and facilitating liquidity in capital markets.

Exploring financing strategies encompasses a wide spectrum of approaches, each with unique benefits, risks, and implications. Effective decision-making requires a deep understanding of the financial landscape, including macroeconomic trends, regulatory frameworks, and investor preferences. Diligent assessment of financing options in alignment with specific objectives, risk tolerance, and market conditions is essential for formulating robust and adaptable financing strategies. Seeking guidance from financial professionals and conducting thorough due diligence can enhance the likelihood of successful outcomes when navigating complex financing landscapes.

Budgeting for maintenance and upkeep

Budgeting for maintenance and upkeep is a critical component of responsible financial management, whether it pertains to personal homeownership, property management, or business operations. This process involves allocating resources to ensure the ongoing care, repair, and preservation of physical assets, infrastructure, and facilities. Let's explore this topic in depth to provide comprehensive insights:

1. Importance of Maintenance Budgeting:

Budgeting for maintenance and upkeep is essential for safeguarding the value and functionality of assets over time. It allows individuals and organizations to plan for routine maintenance, address unexpected repairs, and mitigate the risk of costly asset deterioration. Proactive budgeting for maintenance also supports sustainability efforts by promoting efficient resource utilization and reducing the likelihood of premature asset replacement.

2. Types of Maintenance Expenses:

Maintenance expenses encompass various categories, including preventive maintenance, corrective maintenance, and general upkeep. Preventive maintenance involves scheduled inspections and servicing to prevent equipment or property failures. Corrective maintenance addresses unforeseen breakdowns or damages, requiring immediate repairs. General upkeep encompasses ongoing tasks such as cleaning, landscaping, and minor repairs to preserve the aesthetic and functional aspects of assets.

3. Lifecycle Cost Analysis:

Budgeting for maintenance necessitates a holistic view of asset lifecycle costs, which extend beyond initial acquisition or construction expenses. Conducting a lifecycle cost analysis involves evaluating the total expenses associated with owning, operating, maintaining, and eventually decommissioning or replacing an asset. This approach facilitates informed decision-making regarding long-term budget allocation and capital planning.

4. Reserve Funds for Capital Expenditures:

In addition to routine maintenance budgeting, establishing reserve funds for major capital expenditures is crucial. This entails setting aside funds to address significant asset repairs, replacements, or upgrades that occur less frequently but have substantial financial implications. Examples include replacing a building's roof, upgrading HVAC systems, or refurbishing common areas in a condominium complex.

5. Technology and Data-Driven Maintenance:

Advancements in technology and data analytics have transformed maintenance budgeting practices. Predictive maintenance techniques utilize sensor data, predictive algorithms, and machine learning to forecast equipment failures and optimize maintenance schedules. By harnessing real-time insights, organizations can enhance the efficiency of maintenance operations while minimizing downtime and costly disruptions.

6. Outsourcing vs. In-House Maintenance:

Budgeting considerations extend to evaluating the cost-effectiveness of outsourcing maintenance services versus establishing in-house maintenance teams. Outsourcing may offer specialized expertise, scalability, and cost efficiencies through service level agreements. Conversely, in-house maintenance operations provide greater control and alignment with organizational objectives but require significant investment in staffing, training, and equipment.

7. Emergency Fund for Unforeseen Maintenance Needs:

Prudent maintenance budgeting includes provisions for emergency funds to address unforeseen and urgent maintenance requirements. These funds serve as a financial safety net to swiftly respond to critical repairs, minimizing operational disruptions and preventing potential safety hazards or asset damage.

8. Environmental Sustainability and Compliance:

Budgeting for maintenance increasingly incorporates considerations related to environmental sustainability and regulatory compliance. Investments in energy-efficient upgrades, waste management initiatives, and sustainable materials contribute to operational cost savings and environmental stewardship. Compliance with building codes, health and safety regulations, and environmental standards also informs maintenance budgeting priorities.

In summary, budgeting for maintenance and upkeep demands a comprehensive and forward-thinking approach. It involves balancing short-term operational needs with long-term asset preservation and resilience. Rigorous planning, data-driven insights, and a proactive mindset are essential for optimizing maintenance budget allocation and maximizing the value and longevity of physical assets. Adhering to best practices in maintenance budgeting empowers individuals and organizations to effectively manage risks, enhance operational efficiency, and uphold the quality and functionality of their properties and facilities.

Chapter 4

Building a diverse portfolio

Building a diverse portfolio is a fundamental and time-tested strategy for managing investment risk, maximizing long-term returns, and achieving resilience in the face of market uncertainties. Diversification involves the strategic allocation of investments across various asset classes, with the aim of reducing the impact of individual market fluctuations and specific risks that may affect any single sector or asset. Let's delve deeper into this topic to provide a more comprehensive understanding of the importance and principles of building a diverse investment portfolio.

1. Importance of Diversification:

Diversification is vital for mitigating risk and optimizing returns. By spreading investments across different assets and sectors, investors can reduce the impact of volatility and potential losses associated with any single investment. This risk reduction aspect is particularly crucial during periods of market turbulence, economic downturns, or shifts within specific industries or regions.

2. Asset Allocation Strategies:

Effective diversification begins with strategic asset allocation, which involves determining the optimal mix of asset classes based on individual investor profiles, risk tolerance, financial goals, and time horizons. Asset allocation is essential for balancing growth-oriented assets such as equities and real estate with income-generating assets such as bonds and dividend-paying stocks, thereby creating a diversified portfolio that aligns with the investor's objectives.

3. Stocks and Equities:

Including a variety of stocks in a portfolio allows investors to capture the growth potential of individual companies across different industries and market segments. Diversifying within equities involves considering large-cap, mid-cap, and small-cap stocks, as well as exposure to domestic and international markets. Additionally, thematic and sector-based diversification within equity holdings further enhances risk management and potential return opportunities.

4. Bonds and Fixed-Income Securities:

Bonds play a crucial role in providing income stability and managing equity market risk. Diverse fixed-income instruments, including government bonds, corporate bonds, municipal bonds, and inflation-protected securities, offer varying yields, maturities, and credit qualities, contributing to portfolio diversification and risk management.

5. Real Estate and REITs:

Real estate investments, whether through direct property ownership or real estate investment trusts (REITs), offer diversification benefits by providing exposure to physical assets with potential for income generation, inflation protection, and low correlation to traditional financial markets. Geographic diversification within real estate holdings can further enhance overall portfolio resilience.

6. Alternative Investments:

Diversifying into alternative investments such as commodities, hedge funds, private equity, and infrastructure assets introduces non-traditional sources of return and risk diversification. Alternative investments often exhibit limited correlation to public markets, potentially enhancing overall portfolio resilience and providing access to unique investment opportunities.

7. Geographic and Sector Diversification:

Global diversification is critical for mitigating country-specific risks and capitalizing on varying economic cycles and growth trends. Allocating investments across different geographic regions can reduce the impact of regional economic downturns or political instability. Additionally, sector diversification within equity holdings helps guard against industry-specific downturns and technology disruptions, as different sectors may perform differently in response to economic, geopolitical, or societal changes.

8. Risk Management and Long-Term Performance:

Building a diverse portfolio is not solely about minimizing risk; it also aims to optimize long-term performance. Diversification fosters a more stable and resilient portfolio that can withstand market uncertainties and capitalize on opportunities across different market conditions.

9. Regular Portfolio Rebalancing:

Ongoing portfolio monitoring and periodic rebalancing are crucial aspects of maintaining a diverse investment mix. Rebalancing entails adjusting portfolio weights back to target allocations to ensure that the portfolio's risk-return profile remains aligned with the investor's objectives and market conditions. This process allows investors to take profits from investments that have performed well and reallocate them to assets that may be undervalued, thereby maintaining the desired diversification and risk level.

10. Behavioral Finance Considerations:

Diversifying a portfolio also extends to addressing behavioral biases and emotional influences on investment decisions. By embracing diversification principles, investors can avoid overconcentration in popular assets, reduce susceptibility to cognitive biases, and maintain a disciplined, long-term perspective. This approach can help investors stay focused on their long-term wealth accumulation objectives and avoid reactive decision-making driven by short-term market movements.

Building a diverse portfolio is a cornerstone of prudent investment management. It involves the strategic blend of asset classes, geographic exposure, and sector diversification to enhance risk-adjusted returns and cultivate resilience against market uncertainties. A well-diversified portfolio reflects a thoughtful approach to wealth preservation and growth, fostering a balanced and adaptive investment strategy that aligns with an investor's financial objectives and risk tolerance. Embracing the principles of diversification allows investors to position themselves for long-term success while navigating the ever-changing landscape of global financial markets.

Benefits of diversification

Diversification is a fundamental concept in investment management that offers a wide array of benefits to investors seeking to optimize risk-adjusted returns and build resilient portfolios. This strategy entails spreading investments across various asset classes, geographic regions, and industry sectors to mitigate the impact of individual market fluctuations and specific risks that may affect any single investment. Let's delve deep into the topic of diversification and explore its multitude of benefits in detail.

1. Risk Reduction:

Diversification is primarily valued for its ability to reduce investment risk. By holding a mix of assets with different risk-return profiles, investors can decrease the potential impact of adverse events or volatility on their overall portfolio. For instance, during periods of market downturns or economic crises, assets such as bonds and real estate may behave differently than equities, thus cushioning the overall impact on the portfolio's value.

2. Preservation of Capital:

Through diversification, investors aim to preserve capital while seeking opportunities for growth. By spreading investments across multiple asset classes, the likelihood of suffering substantial losses from a single market event or sector-specific downturn is minimized. This approach contributes to maintaining the long-term value of the portfolio and protecting wealth accumulation efforts.

3. Opportunity Capture:

Diversification offers the potential to capture a broad range of investment opportunities. Different asset classes and sectors may perform well under varying economic conditions or market cycles. By having exposure to diverse investments, investors can benefit from potential growth areas while limiting the impact of underperforming assets.

4. Smoother Return Profile:

A well-diversified portfolio can exhibit a more consistent and stable return profile over time. While individual assets or sectors may experience significant price fluctuations, the presence of diverse holdings can help smooth out the overall return pattern, reducing the portfolio's overall volatility and enhancing predictability.

5. Enhanced Risk-Adjusted Returns:

Through effective diversification, investors seek to achieve a balance between risk and return. By carefully allocating investments across different assets, including equities, fixed income, real estate, and alternative investments, they strive to optimize returns for a given level of risk or volatility. This pursuit of enhanced risk-adjusted returns aligns with the principle of maximizing portfolio efficiency and long-term performance.

6. Protection Against Specific Risks:

Diversification helps guard against exposure to specific risks inherent in individual asset classes or industries. For example, within the equity market, diversifying across various sectors such as technology, healthcare, consumer goods, and energy can mitigate the impact of sector-specific risks, ensuring that the performance of the overall portfolio is not disproportionately influenced by the fortunes of any single industry.

7. Geographic Resilience:

Global diversification provides protection against country-specific risks and enables investors to capitalize on differing economic cycles and growth trends across various regions. Allocating investments internationally can reduce vulnerability to regional economic downturns, currency fluctuations, or geopolitical events in any single country or region.

8. Portfolio Stability:

Diversification contributes to portfolio stability by reducing the impact of adverse events in any single investment or market segment. This stability allows investors to maintain a long-term perspective, stay focused on their financial objectives, and avoid making impulsive decisions in response to short-term market movements.

9. Flexibility and Adaptability:

A diversified portfolio offers flexibility and adaptability in response to changing market conditions and evolving investment opportunities. It allows investors to reposition their portfolios by adjusting allocations across different asset classes and sectors, thereby capitalizing on emerging trends while managing risks prudently.

Diversification offers multifaceted benefits to investors by reducing risk, preserving capital, capturing opportunities, and optimizing risk-adjusted returns. This strategy fosters stability, resilience, and adaptability within investment portfolios, aligning with the goal of building sustainable wealth over the long term. By embracing diversification principles, investors can lay a solid foundation for prudent investment management and navigate the complexities of global financial markets with confidence and resilience.

Balancing high and low-risk investments

Balancing high and low-risk investments is a crucial aspect of portfolio construction and asset allocation, aiming to achieve an optimal blend of risk and return that aligns with an investor's financial goals, risk tolerance, and time horizon. This strategy involves carefully allocating assets across a spectrum of investment options, ranging from conservative, lower-risk instruments to more aggressive, higher-risk opportunities. Let's delve deeply into the topic of balancing high and low-risk investments and explore the intricate considerations and potential benefits associated with this approach.

1. Risk Management:

Balancing high and low-risk investments is fundamentally about risk management. By diversifying across a mix of high and low-risk assets, investors seek to mitigate the impact of adverse market movements and specific risks associated with any single investment. Low-risk investments, such as government bonds or high-quality corporate bonds, provide stability and income, while high-risk investments, like growth stocks or venture capital, offer potential for higher returns but come with increased volatility and potential for loss.

2. Diversification Effect:

Integrating high and low-risk investments within a portfolio enhances diversification. Low-risk investments, such as bonds or cash equivalents, generally exhibit lower correlation with equities and other high-risk assets. Therefore, in times of market stress or economic uncertainty, the performance of low-risk holdings may offset potential losses incurred by high-risk investments, contributing to a more balanced and resilient overall portfolio.

3. Return Generation:

High-risk investments have the potential to generate superior long-term returns compared to low-risk assets. By strategically incorporating growth-oriented assets or exposure to emerging markets, investors can harness the power of compounding and capitalize on wealth-building opportunities. The inclusion of low-risk investments provides stability and income, complementing the return potential of high-risk assets and smoothing out the portfolio's overall return profile.

4. Risk-Adjusted Returns:

Balancing high and low-risk investments seeks to optimize risk-adjusted returns. While high-risk investments may offer the allure of greater potential returns, they also carry heightened volatility and downside risk. By integrating lower-risk assets, investors aim to enhance the overall risk-adjusted performance of the portfolio, aligning with the principle of achieving the highest possible return for a given level of risk.

5. Time Horizon Alignment:

The balance between high and low-risk investments should be aligned with an investor's time horizon. For long-term investors, a greater allocation to high-risk, growth-oriented assets may be suitable, as they have more time to weather short-term market fluctuations and benefit from the long-term growth potential. Conversely, investors with shorter time horizons or those seeking income stability may emphasize low-risk, income-generating investments to preserve capital and provide a steady stream of cash flows.

6. Flexibility and Adaptability:

Balancing high and low-risk investments provides flexibility to adapt to changing market conditions and investor preferences. As market dynamics evolve, investors can adjust their portfolio allocations to rebalance risk exposures, capitalize on emerging opportunities, or safeguard against excessive concentration in any single asset class or risk category.

7. Risk Capacity and Tolerance:

The balance between high and low-risk investments should align with an investor's risk capacity and risk tolerance. Risk capacity pertains to an investor's financial ability to withstand market fluctuations and potential losses, considering factors such as age, income, and overall financial situation. Risk tolerance reflects an investor's psychological comfort level with market volatility and the possibility of temporary portfolio declines. Balancing high and low-risk investments aims to strike a harmonious equilibrium that aligns with both dimensions of risk.

8. Long-Term Wealth Preservation:

Balancing high and low-risk investments supports the preservation of long-term wealth. By diversifying across different risk categories, investors seek to protect capital, generate sustainable returns, and navigate market cycles with prudence and resilience. This long-term perspective underscores the importance of maintaining a balanced and diversified investment approach, leveraging the interplay between high and low-risk assets to promote enduring wealth preservation and growth.

The strategic balance between high and low-risk investments is a cornerstone of effective portfolio management, encompassing risk management, return generation, diversification, and alignment with investor preferences and financial objectives. By integrating a diverse array of high and low-risk assets, investors can construct portfolios that harness the benefits of both risk categories, fostering resilience, stability, and the pursuit of long-term financial success.

Incorporating Real Estate Investment Trusts (REITs)

Real Estate Investment Trusts (REITs) are a type of company that owns, operates, or finances income-generating real estate. These companies have become increasingly popular with investors due to their potential for providing steady income and long-term capital appreciation. Incorporating REITs into an investment portfolio can offer several benefits, but it is important to understand the intricacies of these investments before making any decisions.

1. Understanding REITs:

REITs were created in the United States in 1960 to give individual investors access to income-producing real estate investments. By law, REITs must distribute at least 90% of their taxable income to shareholders annually in the form of dividends. This requirement makes REITs an attractive option for income-seeking investors. Additionally, many REITs are publicly traded on major stock exchanges, making them easily accessible to individual investors.

2. Types of REITs:

There are several types of REITs, including equity REITs, mortgage REITs (mREITs), and hybrid REITs. Equity REITs own and operate income-producing real estate, while mREITs provide financing for income-producing real estate by purchasing or originating mortgages and mortgage-backed securities. Hybrid REITs combine the characteristics of both equity and mortgage REITs.

3. Benefits of Incorporating REITs:

A. Diversification: REITs offer diversification benefits to an investment portfolio. Since they typically have low correlations with stocks and bonds, adding REITs to a portfolio can help spread risk.

B. Income Generation: The 90% income distribution requirement means that REITs often provide higher dividend yields than many other types of investments, making them attractive for income-focused investors.

C. Potential for Capital Appreciation: In addition to dividends, REITs can generate capital appreciation through property value increases and strategic management of real estate assets.

4. Risks to Consider:

A. Interest Rate Sensitivity: REITs can be sensitive to changes in interest rates, which can affect their cost of financing and the attractiveness of their dividend yields relative to other income-generating investments.

B. Economic Downturns: Real estate markets can be cyclical, and REITs may be vulnerable to downturns in the economy or real estate market, potentially leading to declines in property values and rental income.

5. Incorporating REITs into an Investment Portfolio:

When incorporating REITs into an investment portfolio, investors should consider their investment objectives, risk tolerance, and time horizon. A well-diversified portfolio may include a mix of asset classes, such as stocks, bonds, and alternative investments like REITs. It is important to assess the potential impact of REITs on portfolio risk and return characteristics.

6. How to Invest in REITs:

Investors can access REITs through various channels, including individual stock purchases, exchange-traded funds (ETFs) that focus on REITs, and mutual funds that specialize in real estate securities. Each approach has its advantages and considerations, and investors should evaluate fees, liquidity, and diversification when choosing how to invest in REITs.

Incorporating REITs into an investment portfolio can offer diversification, income, and potential for capital appreciation, but it is essential for investors to conduct thorough research and understand the specific characteristics and risks associated with these investments. Due diligence and consultation with a financial advisor can help investors make informed decisions about incorporating REITs into their investment strategy.

Chapter 5

Navigating the Buying Process in Real Estate

Navigating the buying process in real estate involves understanding and managing the various steps and considerations involved in purchasing a property. Here are some key aspects to consider:

1. Steps in the Real Estate Purchase:

- Determine your budget and get pre-approved for a mortgage: Understanding your financial capabilities is fundamental to the homebuying process. Getting pre-approved for a mortgage involves providing financial documentation to a lender, who then assesses your creditworthiness and determines the amount you can borrow.

- Find a real estate agent: A reputable and experienced agent can offer valuable guidance throughout the entire buying journey. Their expertise in market trends, property evaluation, and negotiation skills can be instrumental in finding the right property at the best price.

- Search for properties: Once you have a clear understanding of your budget and the type of property you're looking for, your agent can assist in the search process. In addition to online listings, they may have access to off-market properties and can schedule viewings at convenient times.

- Make an offer: When you find a property that meets your criteria, your agent will help you craft a compelling offer. In this stage, it's essential to consider various factors, such as the current market conditions, comparable property prices, and any specific contingencies.

- Conduct due diligence: Before finalizing the purchase, thorough due diligence is critical. This includes conducting a home inspection to identify any potential issues or repairs needed, reviewing the property's title history to ensure there are no legal encumbrances, and examining any relevant homeowners' association regulations or neighborhood restrictions.

2. Negotiation Techniques for Buyers:

- Understand the market: Gaining insights into the local real estate market's dynamics, including average property prices, demand-supply ratios, and recent sales data, provides a strategic advantage during negotiations.

- Start with a reasonable offer: Crafting an initial offer that reflects the property's value while allowing room for negotiations can set a positive tone with the seller and demonstrate your sincerity as a buyer.

- Be prepared to compromise: Flexibility and openness to compromises can contribute to successful negotiations. Understanding your priorities and where you can be flexible can help navigate the give-and-take of the negotiation process.

- Use a professional real estate agent: The experience and negotiation prowess of a skilled agent can be invaluable. They can leverage their expertise to present offers effectively, navigate counteroffers, and advocate for your interests while maintaining a professional rapport with the seller's representatives.

3. Due Diligence and Property Inspection:

- Home inspection: Engaging a qualified home inspector to scrutinize the property for structural, mechanical, and safety-related issues is crucial. This assessment can reveal potential concerns that may impact the property's value or safety.

- Reviewing documents: Thoroughly reviewing all documentation related to the property, including the title report, survey, and any necessary disclosures, ensures that you have a comprehensive understanding of the property's legal and ownership status.

- Understanding zoning and regulations: Familiarizing yourself with local zoning ordinances and regulations helps you grasp any restrictions on property use, potential future developments in the area, and other relevant considerations.

- Environmental concerns: Assessing environmental factors, such as soil contamination, flood zones, or endangered species habitats, is essential, especially if the property is in an environmentally sensitive area.

By paying attention to these components and engaging professional assistance when needed, navigating the real estate buying process becomes more manageable and can lead to a successful and satisfying property purchase.

Chapter 6

Effective Property Management

Effective property management refers to the successful oversight and operation of real estate assets to achieve the owner's investment objectives. It involves a wide range of responsibilities, including marketing the property, tenant screening and selection, lease administration, financial management, maintenance and repairs, tenant relations, and legal compliance. The goal of effective property management is to maximize the property's value, ensure consistent income, maintain positive tenant relations, and adhere to relevant laws and regulations. Ultimately, effective property management aims to optimize the performance and long-term success of the property while meeting the needs of both property owners and tenants.

Effective property management is essential for property owners and landlords to maximize the value and profitability of their real estate investments. It involves a range of tasks and responsibilities aimed at ensuring the smooth operation, maintenance, and successful leasing or renting of properties. Here are some key aspects of effective property management:

1. Tenant Screening and Selection:

Effective tenant screening and selection are crucial to ensure the long-term success and profitability of a rental property. Here are some key considerations:

- Background checks: Conducting background checks on prospective tenants can help assess their credit history, employment stability, and rental history. This information gives insight into their ability to pay rent on time and maintain a good tenancy.

- Rental application process: Implementing a thorough rental application process ensures you gather all the necessary information from potential tenants. This may include personal information, employment details, references, and consent for background checks.

- Interviewing prospective tenants: Meeting with prospective tenants provides an opportunity to evaluate their personality, communication skills, and suitability for the property. It's essential to ask relevant questions while adhering to fair housing laws.

- Reference checks: Contacting previous landlords or personal references helps verify the accuracy of the information provided by the applicant. This step can provide valuable insights into the potential tenant's behavior and reliability.

By conducting comprehensive tenant screening and selection, property managers can mitigate risks associated with delinquent rent payments, property damage, or disturbance to neighbors.

2. Lease Agreement Best Practices:

A well-drafted lease agreement creates a legally binding document that outlines the rights and responsibilities of both the landlord and tenant. Here are some best practices for lease agreements:

- Clear and concise language: The lease agreement should be written in plain and understandable language, avoiding complex legal jargon. This prevents confusion and ensures both parties fully comprehend their obligations.

- Detailed terms and conditions: The agreement should include essential clauses such as rent payment terms, security deposit details, maintenance responsibilities, rules regarding pets or smoking, lease duration, late fees, and notice requirements for termination or renewal.

- Compliance with local laws: It is imperative to comply with applicable federal, state, and local laws when drafting a lease agreement. This includes adhering to fair housing regulations, tenant rights laws, and any specific rental regulations in the area.

- Professional review: Property managers may consider having legal professionals review their lease agreements to ensure compliance with local regulations and to protect their interests.

By implementing lease agreement best practices, property managers can establish a clear framework for the landlord-tenant relationship, minimize disputes, and safeguard their investment.

3. Property Maintenance and Value Enhancement:

Maintaining the condition of the property and finding ways to enhance its value are crucial aspects of effective property management. Consider the following:

- Regular inspections: Regularly assessing the condition of the property through inspections allows managers to identify maintenance issues and take prompt action, preventing minor problems from becoming major ones.

- Responsive repairs and maintenance: Timely response to tenant repair requests and proactive maintenance measures help maintain tenant satisfaction and prevent further deterioration of the property. Outsourcing routine maintenance tasks to qualified professionals can ensure quality workmanship.

- Upgrades and renovations: Identifying opportunities for property enhancements, such as upgrading appliances, improving landscaping, or updating outdated features, can attract high-quality tenants and potentially increase rental income.

- Building positive relationships with contractors: Establishing relationships with reliable contractors, vendors, and suppliers is beneficial for obtaining competitive prices and ensuring quality services when maintenance or repairs are required.

- Monitoring market trends: Staying informed about market trends in your area can help identify opportunities to increase rental income, such as adjusting rents in response to market demand or offering additional amenities.

By prioritizing property maintenance and seeking strategic value enhancement opportunities, property managers can preserve the value of the property, attract quality tenants, and maximize returns on their investment.

Chapter 7

Maximizing Returns

Maximizing returns in real estate investment involves a multifaceted approach aimed at optimizing the financial performance of the investment. This can involve various strategies and tactics to increase the overall return on investment (ROI) over time.

One key aspect of maximizing returns is increasing rental income. This can be achieved through effective property management, strategic marketing to attract high-quality tenants, and adjusting rental rates in line with market conditions. Additionally, enhancing the property through renovations or improvements can justify higher rental rates, thereby boosting income.

Another crucial element is reducing expenses. This may involve negotiating better terms with service providers, implementing cost-saving measures, and efficiently managing property maintenance and repairs. By minimizing operational costs, investors can improve the property's cash flow and ultimately increase returns.

Minimizing vacancy rates is also essential for maximizing returns. Keeping properties occupied through effective tenant retention strategies and proactive marketing efforts can ensure a steady stream of rental income, thus avoiding revenue loss during periods of vacancy.

Furthermore, optimizing property value appreciation is important for long-term returns. This can be achieved through smart investment in upgrades and enhancements that add value to the property, as well as staying informed about local market trends and making strategic decisions based on potential for appreciation.

Overall, maximizing returns in real estate investment requires a comprehensive and proactive approach that considers various factors such as rental income, expenses, vacancy rates, and property value appreciation, all working together to achieve the goal of maximizing profitability.

Rental Income Strategies

Enhancing rental income involves a multifaceted approach. Investors can conduct thorough market research to identify optimal rental rates and understand tenant demand. In addition, cost reduction strategies such as energy-efficient upgrades, smart management practices, and proactive maintenance can help improve the property's financial performance. Moreover, providing additional amenities, enhancing property appeal, and improving overall service quality can result in increased demand and justify higher rental rates.

Effective rental income strategies are key to maximizing profitability in real estate investment. Here are some valuable strategies to optimize rental income and increase returns:

1. Market Research and Competitive Pricing: Conduct thorough market research to understand the demand and supply dynamics in the local rental market. Analyze comparable properties to determine competitive rental rates. Setting the right rental price is crucial for attracting tenants and maximizing income.

2. Property Upgrades and Amenities: Invest in property upgrades and amenities that can justify higher rental rates. Renovations, modern appliances, and desirable features such as in-unit laundry or outdoor space can

add significant value and allow for increased rent.

3. Targeted Marketing and Tenant Screening: Implement targeted marketing efforts to attract high-quality tenants who are willing to pay a premium for a well-maintained property. Conduct thorough tenant screenings to ensure reliable and financially stable renters, reducing the risk of income loss due to non-payment or property damage.

4. Lease Term Optimization: Consider offering flexible lease terms such as short-term rentals or furnished units to cater to different tenant preferences. Longer lease terms can provide stability and reduce turnover costs, while shorter terms can allow for periodic rent adjustments in response to market conditions.

5. Proactive Property Management: Efficient property management practices can lead to higher rental income. Promptly addressing

maintenance issues, providing excellent customer service, and cultivating positive tenant relationships can contribute to tenant retention and satisfaction, leading to consistent rental income.

6. Ancillary Income Streams: Explore opportunities to generate additional income from the property, such as offering parking spaces, storage units, or pet fees. Implementing smart utility billing strategies, where applicable, can also help offset expenses and increase overall rental income.

7. Rent Increases and Lease Renewals: Regularly review rental rates in line with market trends and consider periodic rent increases when justified by value-added improvements or prevailing market conditions. Encourage lease renewals by maintaining open communication and offering incentives to loyal tenants.

8. Expense Management: Efficiently managing operational expenses can help maximize net rental income. Negotiate favorable terms with service providers, minimize vacancy periods, and implement cost-saving measures without compromising the quality of property maintenance and management.

By implementing these rental income strategies, real estate investors can position their properties for optimal financial performance, ultimately enhancing the overall return on investment.

House Flipping Techniques:

House flipping, the practice of buying distressed properties, renovating them, and selling them quickly for a profit, has gained popularity in the real estate investment industry. To ensure a successful house flipping venture, here are some essential techniques to consider:

1. Thorough Market Research: Before diving into any house flipping project, conduct thorough market research to identify areas with high potential for return on investment. Analyze factors such as local property values, market trends, and demand for renovated homes.

2. Finding Undervalued Properties: Look for distressed properties that can be purchased at a below-market value. These may include foreclosures, short sales, or properties in need of significant repairs. Utilize online listing platforms, real estate agents, or networking with industry professionals to identify potential opportunities.

3. Accurate Financial Analysis: Perform meticulous financial analysis to determine the cost of the property, estimated renovation expenses, and potential selling price.

Consider all the costs involved, including acquisition costs, holding costs (such as taxes, utilities, and insurance), and closing costs.

4. Renovation Strategy: Develop a well-defined renovation strategy to maximize the property's value. Focus on essential upgrades that add significant value, such as kitchen and bathroom remodeling, flooring improvements, or enhancing curb appeal. Prioritize cost-effective renovations that have high impact.

5. Efficient Project Management: Effective project management is crucial for completing the renovation within the allotted time frame and budget. Create a detailed timeline with clearly defined milestones, and closely monitor progress to address any delays or issues promptly.

6. Strategic Marketing: As the renovation nears completion, develop a strategic

marketing plan to attract potential buyers. Utilize professional photography, virtual tours, and staging techniques to highlight the property's best features. Leverage online listing platforms, social media, and networking to reach a wide audience.

7. Pricing Strategy: Set the sale price strategically by considering recent comparable sales in the area, market conditions, and the property's unique features. Find the balance between maximizing profits and attracting potential buyers within a reasonable timeframe.

8. Speedy Sales Process: Aim to sell the property quickly to minimize holding costs and maximize returns. Work with experienced real estate agents or investors who specialize in fast transactions. Ensure all necessary documentation is prepared to facilitate a smooth and efficient closing process.

9. Risk Mitigation: House flipping inherently involves some level of risk. Mitigate risks by conducting thorough due diligence on the property, obtaining appropriate inspections, securing permits for renovations, and having contingency plans in place for unforeseen challenges.

10. Continuous Learning: Stay updated with industry trends, regulations, and best practices through ongoing learning and networking. Attend seminars, workshops, or join real estate investment associations to gain insights from experienced flippers.

Successful house flipping requires a combination of market knowledge, financial acumen, renovation expertise, and effective project management skills. By applying these techniques and continuously refining your approach, you can increase your chances of achieving profitable returns on your house flipping ventures.

Leveraging Tax Incentives:

Tax incentives play a significant role in encouraging certain behaviors or investments, and understanding how to leverage them effectively can provide substantial financial benefits. Whether it's through tax credits, deductions, or incentives for specific activities, here are some key strategies for maximizing opportunities for financial growth through tax incentives:

1. Research and Understanding: Begin by conducting thorough research to identify the tax incentives available at the federal, state, and local levels. These incentives may target various areas such as renewable energy investments, historic property renovations, research and development activities, or investments in designated opportunity zones. Understand the eligibility criteria and requirements associated with each incentive.

2. Consultation with Tax Professionals: Given the complexity of tax laws and regulations, it's crucial to seek guidance from qualified tax professionals or advisors with expertise in the specific incentive areas. They can provide valuable insights into how to structure your investments or activities to maximize tax benefits while ensuring compliance with relevant laws.

3. Strategic Business Planning: For businesses, integrating tax incentives into strategic planning can lead to significant cost savings and improved cash flow. Analyze the potential impact of tax credits, deductions, or deferrals on your business operations and consider how to align your activities with the available incentives.

4. Real Estate Investment and Development: In the real estate industry, tax incentives can be particularly advantageous. Examples include the Low-Income Housing Tax Credit

(LIHTC) for affordable housing projects, Historic Rehabilitation Tax Credits for renovating historic properties, and Opportunity Zone tax benefits for investments in economically distressed communities. Leveraging these incentives can enhance the financial viability of real estate projects.

5. Renewable Energy and Sustainability Initiatives: Tax incentives for renewable energy investments, energy-efficient upgrades, and sustainability initiatives can provide substantial financial benefits. These incentives may include investment tax credits (ITC) for solar, wind, and other renewable energy projects, as well as deductions for energy-efficient building improvements.

6. Research and Development (R&D) Tax Credits: Companies engaged in innovative product development, process improvements, or technological

advancements may be eligible for R&D tax credits. These credits can offset a portion of the expenses incurred in qualifying R&D activities, providing an incentive for companies to invest in innovation.

7. Compliance and Documentation: To fully capture the benefits of tax incentives, it's essential to maintain accurate records, documentation, and compliance with all applicable regulations. This includes diligently tracking expenses, documenting eligible activities, and adhering to any reporting requirements.

8. Legislative Updates and Changes: Stay informed about changes in tax legislation and regulations, as incentives may be revised, extended, or phased out over time. Being aware of legislative updates enables proactive planning to capitalize on available incentives.

9. Community Engagement and Social Impact: Some tax incentives are designed to

encourage community involvement and social impact initiatives. By aligning business activities with these incentives, organizations can not only generate financial benefits but also contribute to meaningful societal causes.

10. Long-Term Financial Planning: When incorporating tax incentives into financial planning, consider the long-term implications and synergies with other financial strategies. Tax-advantaged investments and activities can complement broader wealth management and retirement planning goals.

By strategically leveraging tax incentives, individuals, businesses, and investors can enhance their financial positions, support targeted initiatives, and drive economic growth. Properly navigating the complex landscape of tax incentives requires a comprehensive understanding of applicable laws, proactive planning, and ongoing evaluation of opportunities for optimization.

Chapter 8

Addressing Challenges and Risks:

Challenges and risks refer to potential obstacles, uncertainties, or threats that individuals, organizations, or entities may encounter in the pursuit of their goals or objectives. These challenges and risks can arise from various sources, including internal factors such as organizational processes or external factors like market disruptions, technological advancements, regulatory changes, natural disasters, or economic uncertainties.

Challenges typically signify difficult or demanding situations that require effort, skills, or resources to overcome. They may arise due to factors such as competition, limited resources, changing customer needs, or complex problems that need resolution.

On the other hand, risks generally refer to potential threats or negative outcomes that could affect the achievement of desired outcomes. Risks may arise from factors like financial volatility, security breaches, legal issues, operational failures, reputational damage, or non-compliance with regulations. They have the potential to result in adverse consequences, such as financial loss, damage to reputation, disruption of operations, or harm to stakeholders.

Both challenges and risks are inherent in various facets of life, including business, personal endeavors, and societal contexts. Effectively addressing and managing challenges and risks requires proactive planning, careful assessment, and implementation of appropriate strategies to mitigate, mitigate, transfer, or avoid these potential obstacles and uncertainties.

Challenges and risks are a part of life, with businesses, organizations, and individuals facing various types of risks on a daily basis. In today's complex and dynamic environment, effective risk management is essential to ensure that potential threats do not escalate into significant problems or crises. Here are some strategies for addressing challenges and risks:

1. Identify and Assess Risks: Begin by identifying potential risks and assessing their significance and likelihood of occurrence. This requires a comprehensive understanding of internal and external factors that can affect operations, customers, employees, and other stakeholders. Conducting regular risk assessments and monitoring emerging risks

enables proactive planning and timely mitigation measures.

2. Develop a Risk Management Plan: Based on the identified risks, develop a risk management plan that outlines the strategies and actions needed to mitigate, transfer, or avoid risks. This plan should include detailed procedures and protocols for responding to specific risk scenarios to ensure swift and efficient resolution.

3. Assign Roles and Responsibilities: Clearly assign roles and responsibilities for risk management to ensure that everyone understands their role in implementing the risk management plan. This includes establishing an incident response team or crisis management team to manage risks and respond to emergencies.

4. Establish Policies and Procedures: Develop and implement policies and procedures that address specific risk

scenarios and define the steps needed to mitigate or prevent risks. These policies and procedures should be reviewed and updated regularly to keep pace with evolving risks and changing circumstances.

5. Regular Training and Awareness: Ensure that all employees receive regular training and awareness sessions on risk management, including how to identify, report, and respond to risks. Regular drills and simulations can help employees stay prepared and reduce the impact of a crisis when it occurs.

6. Cybersecurity and Data Protection: With the proliferation of digital technologies and increasing cyber threats, cybersecurity and data protection have become critical risk areas. Ensure that adequate measures are in place to protect sensitive information and systems from unauthorized access and cyber-attacks.

7. Financial Risk Management: Financial risks, including credit risks and market risks, can significantly impact an organization or individual's bottom line. Implement strategies to manage financial risks such as diversifying investments, hedging, and insurance coverage.

8. Continuous Monitoring and Evaluation: Effective risk management requires ongoing monitoring and evaluation of risk management strategies to ensure that they remain relevant and effective. Regularly review risk assessments, incident reports, and other data to identify improvements and adjust risk management plans accordingly.

9. Communication and Stakeholder Engagement: Effective communication and stakeholder engagement are critical to minimizing the impact of a crisis or risk scenario. Establish clear lines of communication with internal and external

stakeholders and keep them informed about risk management efforts and response plans.

10. Compliance and Regulatory Requirements: Ensure compliance with applicable laws and regulations related to risk management. Failure to comply with legal obligations can lead to significant penalties and reputational damage.

Effective risk management is an ongoing process that requires a proactive approach to identify, assess, and address risks. By implementing these strategies, businesses, organizations, and individuals can mitigate risks and build greater resilience to handle unexpected challenges and crises.

Mitigating market fluctuations

Mitigating market fluctuations is a critical concern for businesses that operate in industries that are subject to volatile market conditions. Economic instability, changing consumer preferences, global trade disruptions, and other factors can impact demand, supply, and pricing in a given market, leading to significant fluctuations in sales and revenue. Mitigating these fluctuations is essential to ensure the sustainability and profitability of a business.

To mitigate market fluctuations, businesses need to adopt a proactive approach that involves:

1. Diversifying the product portfolio: One way to mitigate market fluctuations is to diversify the product portfolio. Offering a range of products that cater to different customer segments can help businesses reduce their reliance on a single product or

market, thereby mitigating the risk of significant fluctuations in demand.

2. Building strong customer relationships: Developing strong customer relationships through effective marketing and communication strategies can help businesses maintain customer loyalty and retention, even during market downturns. This can help mitigate the impact of market fluctuations on sales.

3. Forecasting and planning: Effective forecasting and planning can help businesses identify potential market fluctuations, enabling them to prepare for changing market conditions proactively. Businesses can use predictive analytics and other tools to forecast demand, identify trends, and develop contingency plans.

4. Flexibility in operations: Flexibility in operations is crucial to mitigating market fluctuations. Businesses that can quickly

adjust their production, inventory, and pricing strategies can adapt to changes in market conditions, reducing the impact of market fluctuations on their operations.

5. Strategic partnerships and collaborations: Building strategic partnerships and collaborations with other businesses or organizations can help mitigate the impact of market fluctuations. This can involve alliances with suppliers, distributors, or other stakeholders to share resources or collaborate on marketing efforts.

Overall, mitigating market fluctuations requires a comprehensive approach that involves diversification, customer relationship management, forecasting, flexibility in operations, and strategic partnerships. By adopting these strategies, businesses can reduce the impact of market volatility and ensure their long-term success and profitability.

Managing Economic Downturns

Economic downturns, characterized by a general decline in economic activity, can present significant challenges for businesses, individuals, and governments. These downturns can manifest as recessions, depressions, or financial crises, and they often lead to reduced consumer spending, increased unemployment, and financial instability. Managing economic downturns effectively requires a combination of proactive measures and strategic decision-making to mitigate the impact and position organizations for resilience and recovery.

1. Financial Prudence: During economic downturns, it is crucial for businesses to prioritize financial prudence. This includes

closely monitoring cash flow, reducing unnecessary expenses, and optimizing working capital. Maintaining a strong financial position can help businesses weather the downturn and position themselves for future growth.

2. Strategic Cost Management: Implementing cost-cutting measures without sacrificing long-term sustainability is essential. This may involve renegotiating contracts with suppliers, optimizing inventory levels, and streamlining operations to enhance efficiency. Additionally, businesses can explore outsourcing non-core functions to reduce overhead costs.

3. Customer Focus: Maintaining a strong focus on customer satisfaction and retention is vital during economic downturns. Understanding customer needs and adapting products or services accordingly can help businesses retain market share and potentially

gain a competitive edge. Offering value-added solutions and maintaining open lines of communication with customers can foster loyalty and trust.

4. Diversification and Innovation: Exploring new markets, product lines, or revenue streams can help mitigate the impact of economic downturns. Businesses should consider diversifying their offerings to appeal to evolving customer demands and leveraging innovation to stay ahead of the competition. This may involve investing in research and development to create new products or services that address changing market needs.

5. Talent Management: Retaining key talent and fostering employee morale is instrumental in navigating economic downturns. Open communication, transparency, and providing opportunities for upskilling or cross-training can help boost

employee engagement and productivity. Additionally, businesses should prioritize maintaining a positive organizational culture to support their workforce through challenging times.

6. Government Support and Advocacy: Engaging with local, regional, and national government entities to understand available support programs, incentives, or funding opportunities can provide valuable resources for businesses facing economic challenges. Advocacy efforts aimed at influencing economic policies or securing favorable regulatory conditions can also play a role in managing downturns.

7. Scenario Planning and Risk Mitigation: Developing contingency plans and conducting scenario analyses can help businesses prepare for potential outcomes of economic downturns. This involves assessing various risk factors, such as supply chain

disruptions, market volatility, and regulatory changes, and implementing strategies to mitigate associated risks.

Managing economic downturns necessitates a proactive and multifaceted approach that encompasses financial prudence, strategic cost management, customer focus, diversification, talent management, government engagement, and robust risk mitigation. By embracing these strategies, businesses can enhance their resilience, adaptability, and long-term sustainability amidst challenging economic conditions.

Strategies for Handling Property Challenges

Property challenges can encompass a wide range of issues that property owners, investors, and managers may encounter. These may include fluctuations in property value, tenant vacancies, maintenance issues, regulatory changes, and economic downturns. Effectively managing these challenges requires strategic planning, proactive measures, and adaptability to ensure the long-term viability and profitability of real estate assets.

1. Diversification and Portfolio Analysis:

- Diversifying the property portfolio across different asset types and locations can help mitigate risks associated with market fluctuations. Conducting thorough portfolio analysis to identify underperforming assets and reallocating resources can optimize the overall portfolio performance.

2. Proactive Maintenance and Asset Management:

- Implementing proactive maintenance schedules and adhering to asset management best practices can help preserve property value and minimize potential issues. Regular inspections, predictive maintenance techniques, and leveraging technology for efficient property management are essential for maintaining asset quality.

3. Tenant Retention and Satisfaction:

- Focusing on tenant satisfaction and retention strategies is vital for reducing vacancy rates and ensuring steady rental income. This involves responsive communication, addressing tenant concerns promptly, and providing amenities and services that enhance the tenant experience.

4. Financial Planning and Risk Management:

- Developing comprehensive financial plans, including cash flow forecasting, budgeting, and contingency reserves, is crucial for navigating property challenges. Additionally, mitigating risks through property insurance, effective lease structuring, and compliance with regulatory requirements can safeguard against potential financial setbacks.

5. Market Research and Adaptation:

- Staying abreast of market trends, demand dynamics, and regulatory changes is essential for making informed property management decisions. Adapting property offerings to align with evolving market demands, such as implementing sustainability features or technology upgrades, can enhance property appeal and competitiveness.

6. Relationship Building and Networking:

- Establishing strong relationships with industry professionals, local authorities, and service providers can provide valuable support in addressing property challenges.

Networking opportunities can facilitate knowledge sharing, access to resources, and potential collaborations for property improvement initiatives.

7. Legal Compliance and Risk Mitigation:

- Ensuring compliance with applicable property laws, zoning regulations, environmental requirements, and safety standards is critical for mitigating legal risks. Engaging legal counsel as needed and maintaining stringent adherence to compliance protocols can protect property interests and reputation.

Implementing these strategies for handling property challenges requires a comprehensive and proactive approach that encompasses diversification, maintenance, tenant satisfaction, financial planning, market adaptation, relationship building, and risk mitigation. By leveraging these strategies, property owners and managers can navigate challenges effectively, optimize property performance, and position their portfolios for long-term success in the dynamic real estate landscape.

Chapter 9

Legal and Regulatory Considerations

In the realm of property ownership, management, and investment, navigating legal and regulatory considerations is paramount to ensure compliance, mitigate risks, and uphold the integrity of real estate assets. Understanding and adhering to applicable laws, regulations, and best practices is essential for safeguarding property interests, maintaining ethical standards, and fostering a positive relationship with stakeholders. This topic encompasses various aspects, including property laws, zoning regulations, landlord-tenant statutes, environmental mandates, and safety standards, among others.

1. Property Laws:

- Property laws govern the rights, obligations, and transactions related to real estate. These encompass ownership rights, property transfers, title deeds, and regulations pertaining to land use and development. Understanding property laws is crucial for navigating property acquisitions, disposals, and ensuring legal compliance in property management activities.

2. Zoning Regulations:

- Zoning regulations dictate land usage, building codes, and permissible activities within specific geographic areas. Complying with zoning laws is vital for undertaking property development, renovations, and ensuring alignment with designated land use categories to avoid legal ramifications and development restrictions.

3. Landlord-Tenant Statutes:

- Legal frameworks governing landlord-tenant relationships address lease agreements, rental payments, eviction procedures, tenant rights, and property maintenance responsibilities. Adhering to relevant landlord-tenant statutes is essential for maintaining harmonious and lawful interactions with tenants while protecting property owner rights.

4. Environmental Mandates:

- Environmental regulations encompass considerations such as hazardous materials, pollution control, waste management, and conservation efforts. Property owners and developers must comply with environmental mandates to mitigate potential liabilities, address contamination issues, and contribute to sustainable property practices.

5. Safety Standards:

- Adhering to safety standards and building codes is imperative for ensuring the structural integrity, occupant safety, and compliance with fire, health, and accessibility regulations. Property owners and managers are responsible for maintaining safe and habitable premises in accordance with applicable safety standards.

The importance of legal and regulatory considerations cannot be overstated, as non-compliance can lead to legal disputes, financial penalties, reputational damage, and operational disruptions. Property professionals must stay informed about evolving laws, seek legal counsel when needed, and implement robust compliance frameworks to uphold the legal and ethical integrity of their real estate endeavors.

By addressing legal and regulatory considerations conscientiously, property stakeholders can protect their investments, foster transparency and accountability, and contribute to a thriving and compliant real estate ecosystem.

Understanding Real Estate Laws

Real estate laws are legal provisions and regulations that govern the acquisition, ownership, use, and transfer of property. These laws encompass a wide array of statutes, codes, and regulations designed to ensure fairness, transparency, and legality in real estate transactions and activities. Understanding real estate laws is crucial for all parties involved in property transactions, including buyers, sellers, landlords, tenants, developers, and property managers.

1. Property Ownership:

   - Real estate laws define the rights and responsibilities of property ownership, encompassing aspects such as title deeds, easements, boundaries, and property transfer procedures. By understanding these laws, individuals can navigate property acquisitions, transfers, and disputes while safeguarding their ownership rights.

2. Contract Law:

- Contract law is fundamental in real estate transactions, governing the creation, execution, and enforcement of property-related agreements. Understanding the principles of contract law enables parties to negotiate, draft, and execute contracts such as purchase agreements, lease agreements, and property management contracts with clarity and legal compliance.

3. Land Use and Zoning Regulations:

- Real estate laws include regulations that control land use, zoning designations, building codes, and development restrictions. Familiarity with these laws is essential for property developers, investors, and municipal entities to ensure that property development and usage align with regulatory requirements and zoning designations.

4. Landlord-Tenant Laws:

   - Legal frameworks that govern landlord-tenant relationships cover areas such as lease agreements, rent payments, eviction procedures, and tenant rights. Understanding these laws is critical for landlords and tenants to establish fair and lawful rental arrangements, address disputes, and uphold their respective rights and obligations.

5. Environmental Regulations:

   - Environmental laws relevant to real estate pertain to issues such as hazardous materials, pollution control, environmental impact assessments, and conservation measures. Property stakeholders must be aware of these regulations to address environmental liabilities, ensure compliance with environmental standards, and contribute to sustainable property practices.

6. Disclosure Requirements:

- Real estate laws often mandate the disclosure of certain information by sellers, landlords, and real estate agents to prospective buyers or tenants. Understanding these disclosure requirements is vital to avoid legal liabilities and ensure transparency in property transactions.

7. Taxation and Finance Laws:

- Real estate laws encompass taxation regulations, financing rules, and property-related fiscal policies. Individuals involved in real estate transactions must comprehend these laws to navigate tax implications, financing options, and investment strategies effectively.

By comprehensively understanding real estate laws, individuals can make informed decisions, mitigate legal risks, and ensure ethical and legal compliance in their real estate endeavors. Seeking legal counsel, staying updated on relevant legal developments, and adhering to best practices in real estate law is essential for maintaining integrity in property transactions and operations.

In summary, real estate laws form the legal foundation that governs property transactions, ownership rights, and property-related activities. Acquiring a thorough understanding of these laws is essential for fostering confidence, transparency, and legal adherence within the real estate industry.

Navigating Zoning Regulations

Zoning regulations are a critical aspect of real estate law and urban planning, governing the use of land within specific jurisdictions. These regulations divide a municipality into different zones or districts, each with distinct permitted land uses, building requirements, and development standards. Navigating zoning regulations is essential for property owners, developers, and investors to ensure compliance and successful project implementation within a given area.

1. Understanding Zoning Classifications:

   - Zoning regulations typically classify areas into residential, commercial, industrial, and mixed-use zones, among others. Each classification comes with its own set of permitted uses, building heights, setback requirements, parking standards, and other development guidelines. By familiarizing themselves with the zoning classifications, stakeholders can determine the types of activities allowed in a specific area and plan their projects accordingly.

2. Researching Zoning Ordinances and Codes:

- Municipalities have zoning ordinances and codes that detail the specific regulations governing each zoning district. These documents outline the permitted land uses, development standards, setback requirements, building codes, and procedural guidelines for obtaining zoning variances or special permits. Understanding these ordinances is crucial for property owners and developers to ensure that their proposed projects align with local zoning requirements.

3. Seeking Zoning Approvals and Permits:

- When undertaking new construction, renovations, or changes in land use, it is imperative to secure the necessary zoning approvals and permits from the local planning or zoning department. This process often involves submitting site plans, zoning variance applications, or conditional use permits for review and approval. Navigating this process requires a clear understanding of the local zoning regulations and procedural requirements.

4. Engaging with Zoning Authorities and Planners:

- Establishing open communication with zoning authorities, planning departments, and municipal planners can provide valuable insights into zoning regulations and streamline the permitting process. Engaging proactively with these officials allows property owners and developers to seek guidance, address potential zoning issues, and gain clarity on the regulatory framework affecting their properties or projects.

5. Evaluating Zoning Challenges and Opportunities:

- Navigating zoning regulations also involves assessing potential challenges and opportunities associated with specific zoning designations. This includes identifying opportunities for property rezoning, understanding the implications of variances or conditional use permits, and navigating potential conflicts with existing zoning restrictions.

6. Consulting with Legal and Land Use Professionals:

- Given the complexity of zoning regulations, seeking legal counsel and collaborating with land use professionals such as urban planners, architects, and zoning consultants can provide valuable expertise and guidance. These professionals can help interpret zoning regulations, navigate the permitting process, and strategize to achieve project goals within the bounds of regulatory requirements.

Navigating zoning regulations involves a comprehensive understanding of zoning classifications, research into local ordinances, securing necessary approvals and permits, engaging with zoning authorities, assessing challenges and opportunities, and seeking professional expertise. By effectively navigating zoning regulations, property owners and developers can ensure compliance with land use regulations, optimize project feasibility, and contribute to sustainable and well-planned urban development.

Tax implications and strategies

Tax implications and strategies refer to the impact of taxation on various financial decisions and the methods used to minimize tax liability within the boundaries of the law.

Understanding the tax implications of financial activities is essential for individuals, businesses, and investors to make informed decisions and optimize their tax position.

Tax implications can arise in various financial transactions, such as investment income, business operations, real estate transactions, and estate planning. Different forms of income, including wages, interest, dividends, and capital gains, are subject to different tax rates and treatment. Additionally, deductions, credits, and exemptions can affect an individual or company's overall tax liability.

Tax strategies involve proactive planning and decision-making to legally reduce tax burdens. These strategies may include retirement account contributions, charitable donations, capital gains harvesting, tax-loss harvesting, utilizing tax-advantaged accounts, and structuring business transactions in a tax-efficient manner.

Furthermore, tax strategies can also encompass estate planning to minimize estate taxes, succession planning for family businesses, and structuring investments to optimize after-tax returns. It's important to note that tax laws are complex and subject to change, so individuals and businesses should consult with tax professionals to develop and implement effective tax strategies tailored to their specific circumstances.

In summary, understanding tax implications and employing effective tax strategies are crucial for maximizing after-tax wealth and making sound financial decisions. By being mindful of the tax consequences of various actions, individuals and businesses can strive to minimize their tax burden while remaining compliant with tax laws and regulations.

Chapter 10

Long-term wealth building

Long-term wealth building refers to the process of accumulating and growing wealth over an extended period. It involves making strategic financial decisions and adopting disciplined saving and investing practices with the aim of achieving financial independence and stability in the future.

Building long-term wealth requires a comprehensive approach that encompasses several key aspects:

1. Setting Financial Goals: Clearly defining your financial objectives is crucial for effective wealth building. Whether it's saving for retirement, purchasing a home, or funding education, having specific goals helps in

formulating a plan and staying focused on the long-term.

2. Developing a Budget: Creating a budget allows you to track income and expenses, identify areas for potential savings, and allocate funds towards wealth-building strategies. It helps in managing cash flow effectively and ensures that saving and investing become priorities.

3. Saving Consistently: Regular saving is a fundamental element of wealth building. By setting aside a portion of income on a consistent basis, you can gradually accumulate funds over time. It's advisable to automate savings through automatic transfers or payroll deductions to ensure consistency.

4. Investing Wisely: Investing is a crucial component of long-term wealth building as it enables the growth of assets and helps to outpace inflation. Diversification, risk management, and asset allocation are vital

considerations when constructing an investment portfolio. Employing a mix of equities, bonds, real estate, and other investment vehicles can help mitigate risk while striving for long-term growth.

5. Minimizing Debt: Managing and reducing debt is essential for wealth building. High-interest debts, such as credit card debt or loans, can erode wealth-building efforts. Prioritizing debt repayment, avoiding unnecessary borrowing, and maintaining a good credit score are essential to minimize interest expenses and free up cash flow.

6. Continual Learning and Improvement: Staying updated on financial trends, investment strategies, and personal finance best practices is crucial for long-term wealth building. Reading books, attending seminars, seeking professional advice, and learning from successful investors can help refine strategies and enhance financial knowledge.

7. Patience and Discipline: Building long-term wealth requires patience and discipline. The journey towards financial security may include setbacks, market fluctuations, and unexpected events. Maintaining a long-term perspective, staying committed to the plan, and avoiding impulsive decisions are vital for success.

Long-term wealth building is a gradual and strategic process that involves setting goals, saving consistently, investing wisely, managing debt, continuous learning, and exercising patience and discipline. By adopting these principles and taking a proactive approach to personal finance, individuals can work towards achieving financial independence and building a solid foundation for their future.

Retirement planning through real estate

Retirement planning through real estate refers to the process of investing in properties with the goal of achieving long-term financial stability during retirement years. Real estate investment can provide a reliable and steady source of income, asset appreciation, and potential tax benefits that can contribute to a more fulfilling retirement.

Here are some key considerations for using real estate as a retirement planning tool:

1. Choosing the Right Property: When selecting a property for retirement investment, it's essential to consider factors such as location, rental value, and potential for capital appreciation. Properties in desirable areas with strong demand, potential growth prospects, and stable rental income can provide consistent returns over time.

2. Financing Options: Real estate investment for retirement planning can be financed through mortgage loans. It's crucial to assess the affordability of the loan payments, potential rental income, and cash flow projections to ensure profitability. Careful consideration of interest rates, repayment terms, and potential market risks should also be taken into account.

3. Rental Income: Rental income from real estate investment can provide a steady stream of passive income during retirement. It's important to set realistic rental rates, manage tenant relationships professionally, and maintain properties well to ensure consistent rental income.

4. Appreciation Potential: Real estate investment can provide long-term capital appreciation potential. Properties in desirable locations may appreciate in value over time, providing a valuable asset that can be sold or

used to secure loans during retirement. However, it's important to note that market fluctuations can affect the value of real estate assets, and it's crucial to monitor market trends and adjust the portfolio accordingly.

5. Tax Benefits: Real estate investment can provide various tax benefits, including deductions for mortgage interest, operating expenses such as maintenance costs, and depreciation of the property value. It's important to seek advice from tax professionals to understand the tax implications and optimize the investment strategy.

In conclusion, real estate investment is a viable way to plan for retirement by creating a diversified, long-term portfolio of income-generating assets. It's crucial to approach real estate investment for retirement planning with a strategic mindset, considering factors such as property location, financing options, rental income, potential appreciation, and tax benefits. Seeking professional advice and regular monitoring of market trends can help optimize the portfolio and achieve financial stability during retirement years.

Legacy planning and generational wealth

Legacy planning and generational wealth are interconnected concepts that involve intentional actions taken to preserve and transfer wealth from one generation to the next. It focuses on creating a lasting financial legacy that can benefit future generations and provide opportunities for prosperity.

Legacy planning involves a comprehensive approach to estate planning, which goes beyond simply distributing assets upon death. It encompasses strategies and considerations for managing, preserving, and growing wealth over time while also addressing the values, goals, and aspirations of the family.

Here are some key aspects of legacy planning and generational wealth:

1. Estate Planning: Estate planning is a crucial component of legacy planning. It involves creating legal documents, such as wills, trusts, and powers of attorney, to ensure that assets are distributed according to the individual's wishes. Proper estate planning can minimize taxes, avoid probate, and protect assets, ensuring a smooth and efficient transfer of wealth to future generations.

2. Wealth Preservation: Legacy planning includes strategies to preserve and protect wealth. This may involve diversifying investments, managing risks, and implementing measures to mitigate potential threats to the family's financial security. It may also involve reviewing insurance

policies, structuring business entities, and setting up asset protection trusts to safeguard wealth from unforeseen events or lawsuits.

3. Education and Financial Literacy: Educating and imparting financial literacy to future generations is crucial for the long-term success of generational wealth. Providing resources, mentorship, and guidance on financial matters can empower succeeding generations to make wise decisions, manage wealth responsibly, and continue to grow the family's financial legacy.

4. Philanthropy and Charitable Giving: Legacy planning often includes incorporating philanthropy and charitable giving into the family's values and mission. Establishing charitable trusts, foundations, or donor-advised funds can ensure ongoing support for causes that align with the family's values while also providing tax benefits. Engaging the family in charitable endeavors

can promote a sense of purpose, unity, and social impact.

5. Succession Planning: Successful generational wealth transfer requires careful succession planning. This involves identifying potential successors and preparing them to take on leadership roles in managing and growing the family's wealth. It may include professional development, mentorship, and clear communication about the family's vision, values, and expectations.

6. Professional Guidance: Legacy planning and generational wealth management often require the expertise of professionals such as estate planning attorneys, financial advisors, trust officers, and tax specialists. These professionals can provide valuable insights and guidance, helping to ensure that the planning is comprehensive, legally sound, and aligned with the family's objectives.

Legacy planning and generational wealth involve more than just financial planning. They encompass a holistic approach to preserving, growing, and passing on wealth, while also promoting family values, education, philanthropy, and responsible financial management. By taking proactive steps and seeking professional guidance, individuals can create a meaningful legacy that provides for future generations and leaves a positive impact on the world.

Real estate as a passive income source

Real estate is a popular and attractive option for generating passive income. Passive income refers to earnings that require minimal effort and time once the initial investment is made. Real estate provides the potential for steady, reliable, and long-term income streams without actively working a traditional job.

Here are some key aspects of real estate as a passive income source:

1. Rental Properties: One common way to generate passive income through real estate is by purchasing rental properties. By owning and renting out residential or commercial properties, you can earn a consistent stream of rental income. Once the property is acquired and tenants are in place, the income becomes relatively passive, especially if you hire a property management company to handle tenant management, maintenance, and rent collection.

2. Real Estate Investment Trusts (REITs): REITs are companies that own, operate, and manage income-generating real estate properties. By investing in REITs, individuals can passively earn regular dividends and participate in the appreciation of the underlying properties without the need to directly own or manage them. REITs can be

publicly traded on stock exchanges, providing liquidity and ease of investment.

3. Crowdfunding Platforms: Real estate crowdfunding platforms have emerged as a way for individuals to passively invest in real estate projects. These platforms pool funds from various investors to finance real estate developments, such as residential or commercial properties. Investors can enjoy the potential benefits of real estate investment while diversifying their risks and having professionals handle the day-to-day management.

4. Short-term Rentals: The rise of online platforms like Airbnb has made it easier for property owners to generate passive income through short-term rentals. By renting out a spare room or an entire property to travelers, individuals can earn income on a flexible basis. While managing bookings and guests require some involvement, automation and

professional services can help reduce the time and effort required.

5. Real Estate Partnerships: Investing in real estate partnerships or syndications is another way to passively earn income from real estate. These partnerships pool resources and expertise to acquire and manage larger-scale real estate projects, such as apartment complexes, commercial buildings, or storage facilities. Investors can contribute capital and benefit from the cash flow and appreciation generated by the property, relying on the expertise of the partnership manager.

6. Real Estate Royalties: Real estate royalties involve the licensing or leasing of intellectual property related to real estate, such as trademarks, brand names, or proprietary systems. By owning and licensing these rights, individuals can receive passive royalty income from other businesses or individuals who pay to use the intellectual property.

It's important to note that while real estate can provide passive income, it does require upfront capital and due diligence in property selection, financing, and management. Market conditions, location, tenant quality, and property maintenance can impact the profitability of real estate investments. Additionally, legal and tax considerations should be carefully evaluated.

In summary, real estate offers various avenues to generate passive income, including rental properties, REITs, crowdfunding platforms, short-term rentals, partnerships, and royalties. Each method has its own set of advantages, risks, and requirements. By thoroughly researching, planning, and potentially seeking professional guidance, individuals can leverage real estate as a passive income source, diversify their investment portfolio, and build long-term wealth.

Chapter 11

Staying Informed and Adapting

Staying informed and adapting are crucial aspects of leading a successful and fulfilling life. In today's fast-paced, interconnected world, the ability to stay abreast of evolving information, trends, and developments is vital for making well-informed decisions and navigating the ever-shifting landscape of challenges and opportunities.

Whether it's keeping up with global news, industry trends, educational advancements, or technological innovations, actively seeking knowledge and staying informed empowers individuals to expand their understanding of the world around them. This not only facilitates personal growth but also enhances their ability to make impactful contributions to their communities and professions.

Moreover, the concept of adaptation goes hand in hand with staying informed. Embracing change and being open to new ideas, technologies, and ways of doing things fosters resilience and flexibility. It enables individuals to pivot in response to unexpected circumstances, seize opportunities, and remain agile in the face of uncertainty.

By cultivating a mindset of curiosity, openness, and proactivity, individuals can position themselves to thrive in a rapidly changing world. This involves not only consuming information but also critically evaluating it, discerning credible sources, and continuously learning and unlearning as new information becomes available.

In essence, staying informed and adapting are lifelong skills that enable individuals to not only survive but thrive in the dynamic and unpredictable modern environment. By remaining curious, open-minded, and responsive to change, we can tap into our full potential and effectively navigate the complexities of our personal and professional lives.

Keeping Abreast of Market Trends

Keeping abreast of market trends is a critical practice for individuals and businesses alike, as it involves staying informed about shifts, developments, and patterns within specific industries or global markets. This proactive approach allows individuals and organizations to make well-informed decisions, capitalize on emerging opportunities, and adapt to changing conditions. Here's a deeper look into the importance and strategies for keeping abreast of market trends:

1. Research and Analysis:

- Comprehensive research involves delving into industry-specific publications, market reports, and financial news to identify overarching trends, shifts in consumer preferences, and disruptive technologies. This can include examining macroeconomic data and forecasts, as well as examining company-specific reports and financial disclosures.

- Strategic analysis of this information involves understanding the implications of identified trends on various aspects of business operations, such as supply chain management, sales and marketing strategies, and product development.

2. Networking:

- Engaging with industry professionals offers the opportunity to gain firsthand insights into emerging trends, best practices, and potential challenges. It also facilitates the exchange of ideas and fosters collaboration, which can be invaluable in understanding the context and implications of market trends.

- By actively participating in industry events, individuals and businesses can build relationships with key stakeholders and thought leaders, gaining access to exclusive insights and early indicators of market shifts.

3. Technology and Analytics:

- Leveraging advanced technology tools and analytics platforms allows for real-time monitoring and interpretation of market data, consumer behavior, and competitive activities. This enables the identification of subtle yet impactful trends that may not be immediately apparent through traditional research methods.

- The use of artificial intelligence and machine learning algorithms can provide predictive analytics, allowing businesses to anticipate market trends and plan proactive measures accordingly.

4. Consumer Feedback:

- Actively soliciting feedback from customers through surveys, focus groups, and social media engagement provides valuable insights into shifting consumer preferences, emerging needs, and evolving purchasing behaviors. Such feedback can serve as an early warning system for market trends and can inform strategic decision-making.

- Monitoring customer sentiment through sentiment analysis tools and social listening platforms helps in gauging public opinion and capturing nuanced reactions to products, services, or industry developments.

5. Continuous Learning:

- Emphasizing ongoing education and professional development ensures that individuals and organizations are equipped to understand and adapt to changes in regulations, technology, and industry best practices. This can involve attending industry-specific workshops, webinars, and courses to stay informed about the latest trends and developments.

- Keeping abreast of changing regulatory landscapes, geopolitical shifts, and technological advancements is crucial for anticipating how these external factors may influence market trends and business operations.

By implementing these deeply integrated strategies, individuals and businesses can cultivate a comprehensive understanding of market trends, enabling them to respond effectively to evolving conditions and capitalize on emerging opportunities. This depth of understanding empowers proactive decision-making and positions stakeholders to thrive in dynamic and competitive market environments.

Adapting Strategies to Market Changes

In today's dynamic and ever-evolving business landscape, the ability to adapt strategies to market changes is crucial for the long-term success and sustainability of any organization. As markets undergo transformation due to factors such as technological advancements, shifting consumer behaviors, regulatory modifications, or global economic fluctuations, businesses must proactively adjust their approaches to remain competitive and meet the evolving needs of their target audiences. Here are several essential considerations for effectively adapting strategies to market changes:

1. Agility and Flexibility:

- Embracing an agile mindset entails being receptive to change and having the ability to swiftly realign strategies in response to market shifts. Rather than adhering rigidly to predetermined plans, organizations should cultivate a culture of flexibility that allows for rapid adaptation to emerging trends and opportunities.

2. Continuous Monitoring and Analysis:

- Regularly monitoring market dynamics, including consumer trends, competitor activities, and industry developments, is essential for identifying early indicators of change. Through robust data analysis and market research, organizations can gain insights into emerging opportunities and potential threats, enabling informed decision-making.

3. Customer-Centric Approach:

- Adapting strategies to market changes necessitates a deep understanding of evolving consumer preferences, needs, and behaviors. By prioritizing customer feedback, conducting in-depth market segmentation, and leveraging data analytics, businesses can tailor their offerings and experiences to align with shifting market demands.

4. Innovation and Adaptation:

- Embracing innovation as a core component of business strategy enables organizations to proactively anticipate and respond to market changes. This may involve developing new products or services, enhancing existing offerings, or adopting novel business models that resonate with evolving market conditions.

5. Strategic Partnerships and Alliances:

- Collaborating with strategic partners and forging alliances within the industry can enhance an organization's ability to adapt to market changes. By leveraging complementary strengths and resources, businesses can be better positioned to navigate transitions and capitalize on emerging opportunities.

6. Risk Management and Contingency Planning:

- Implementing robust risk management practices and developing contingency plans are essential components of adapting strategies to market changes. Having a clear understanding of potential risks and devising proactive measures to mitigate them bolsters an organization's resilience in the face of market uncertainties.

7. Organizational Alignment and Communication:

- Effective adaptation to market changes requires alignment across all levels of the organization. Clear communication of revised strategies, objectives, and expectations, coupled with ongoing employee engagement, fosters a cohesive and responsive corporate culture capable of embracing change.

8.   Regulatory   and   Compliance Considerations:

- Adapting strategies to market changes entails staying abreast of evolving regulatory requirements and compliance standards. Businesses must remain vigilant to changes in legislation, industry regulations, and geopolitical dynamics, and modify their strategies accordingly to ensure legal and ethical adherence.

By integrating these considerations into their strategic planning and operational frameworks, businesses can better position themselves to thrive amidst market changes. Embracing adaptability as a foundational principle empowers organizations to anticipate, respond to, and capitalize on shifts in the market, ultimately fostering long-term growth and resilience.

Continuing education in real estate

Continuing education in real estate refers to the ongoing learning and professional development that individuals working in the real estate industry pursue to enhance their knowledge, skills, and expertise. As the field of real estate is constantly evolving with changing regulations, market trends, and best practices, continuing education plays a vital role in keeping real estate professionals up-to-date and competent in their roles.

There are several reasons why continuing education is important in the real estate industry:

1. Stay Current with Laws and Regulations: Real estate laws and regulations can change frequently at the local, state, and national

levels. Continuing education ensures that real estate professionals are aware of any updates or amendments to these legal frameworks, allowing them to practice ethically and within legal boundaries.

2. Enhance Professional Competence: Taking part in continuing education programs helps real estate professionals enhance their competence and proficiency in the various aspects of their job. It allows them to develop a deeper understanding of market trends, property management techniques, financing options, negotiation strategies, and other essential skills required for success in the industry.

3. Expand Knowledge Base: Continuing education provides opportunities for real estate professionals to expand their knowledge base beyond their area of specialization. They can explore different sectors of real estate, such as commercial,

residential, industrial, or investment properties, and gain insights into new emerging markets or innovative practices.

4. Maintain Professional Licensing and Designations: Many states and professional organizations require real estate professionals to complete a certain number of continuing education hours to maintain their licenses and designations. This ensures that professionals are consistently updating their knowledge and skills throughout their careers.

5. Networking and Collaboration: Continuing education programs often bring together professionals from diverse backgrounds and experiences. This provides an excellent platform for networking and collaboration, facilitating the exchange of ideas, sharing best practices, and building relationships with fellow industry experts.

6. Adapt to Industry Changes: The real estate industry is subject to constant change due to

factors like technological advancements, economic fluctuations, and shifting buyer preferences. Continuing education equips professionals with the tools and insights needed to adapt to these changes effectively and capitalize on emerging opportunities.

Continuing education in real estate can take various forms, including seminars, workshops, online courses, conferences, and professional designation programs. These programs cover a wide range of topics, such as legal and ethical practices, marketing and sales strategies, property valuation, risk management, property financing, and property development.

Overall, continuing education in real estate is critical for professionals who want to excel in their careers and provide exceptional service to clients. By staying current with industry developments and expanding their knowledge base, real estate professionals can navigate the complexities of the market with confidence and build long-lasting success.

Conclusion

In conclusion, the journey towards ongoing success in the real estate industry requires a commitment to continuous learning and improvement. Throughout this discussion, we have explored several key strategies that are instrumental in achieving long-term success in the field of real estate.

To recap, staying up-to-date with laws and regulations is paramount in ensuring ethical practice and compliance. This not only protects clients but also establishes trust and credibility within the industry. Additionally, enhancing professional competence through continuous education allows real estate professionals to stay ahead of market trends and provide exceptional service to their clients. By continuously expanding their knowledge base, professionals can navigate complex transactions and address the unique needs of their clients effectively.

Furthermore, obtaining and maintaining professional licenses and designations is an essential component of ongoing real estate success. These credentials demonstrate a commitment to professionalism and expertise in specialized areas of the industry. They serve as a testament to one's dedication to personal growth and instill confidence in clients when choosing a real estate professional to work with.

Networking and collaboration opportunities provided by continuing education programs should not be underestimated. Engaging with peers and industry experts allows for the exchange of best practices, valuable insights, and the building of a supportive professional community. Through these connections, real estate professionals can learn from others' experiences, gain fresh perspectives, and foster partnerships that can lead to new business opportunities.

As we come to the end of our discussion, I want to encourage you to embrace ongoing education as a gateway to your continued success in real estate. It is important to approach this journey with an open mind, recognizing that every piece of knowledge gained and skill honed is an investment in your career. Embrace the challenges and opportunities provided by ongoing education, as they will empower you to adapt to changes in the industry and stand out among your peers.

Remember, ongoing success in real estate is not solely about achieving milestones or attaining high sales figures. It is about continuously striving for excellence, keeping abreast of industry developments, and delivering exceptional value to your clients. By cultivating a mindset of continuous learning and improvement, you are positioning yourself for long-term success and fulfillment in the ever-changing world of real estate.

So, go forth with confidence, enthusiasm, and a hunger for knowledge. Let ongoing education be the fuel that propels you towards even greater heights of achievement and impact in the real estate industry. Your dedication to personal growth and professional development will not only benefit you but also leave a lasting legacy in the realm of real estate.

REVIEW PAGE

Dear [Reader],

I hope this message finds you well. We value your opinion and would greatly appreciate it if you could take a moment to share your feedback with us. Your insights are important to us as we continuously strive to enhance our products/services.

Kindly consider leaving a review on our website or preferred platform. Your honest feedback will not only assist us in improving but also guide others in making informed decisions.

Thank you for being a valued member of our community.

Best regards, [John M. Woods]

www.ingramcontent.com/pod-product-compliance
Lightning Source LLC
Chambersburg PA
CBHW072152290526
45794CB00004B/1490